Cambridge Elements

Elements in Writing in the Ancient World
edited by
Andréas Stauder
École Pratique des Hautes Études–PSL (EPHE)

WRITING IN BRONZE AGE CRETE

'Minoan' Linear A

Ester Salgarella
*Aarhus Institute of Advanced Studies,
Aarhus University*

CAMBRIDGE
UNIVERSITY PRESS

Shaftesbury Road, Cambridge CB2 8EA, United Kingdom

One Liberty Plaza, 20th Floor, New York, NY 10006, USA

477 Williamstown Road, Port Melbourne, VIC 3207, Australia

314–321, 3rd Floor, Plot 3, Splendor Forum, Jasola District Centre,
New Delhi – 110025, India

103 Penang Road, #05–06/07, Visioncrest Commercial, Singapore 238467

Cambridge University Press is part of Cambridge University Press & Assessment,
a department of the University of Cambridge.

We share the University's mission to contribute to society through the pursuit of
education, learning and research at the highest international levels of excellence.

www.cambridge.org
Information on this title: www.cambridge.org/9781009520027

DOI: 10.1017/9781009520041

When citing this work, please include a reference to the DOI 10.1017/9781009520041

First published 2025

A catalogue record for this publication is available from the British Library

ISBN 978-1-009-52002-7 Hardback
ISBN 978-1-009-52006-5 Paperback
ISSN 2753-6378 (online)
ISSN 2753-636X (print)

Additional resources for this publication at www.cambridge.org/salgarella

Writing in Bronze Age Crete

'Minoan' Linear A

Elements in Writing in the Ancient World

DOI: 10.1017/9781009520041
First published online: August 2025

Ester Salgarella
Aarhus Institute of Advanced Studies, Aarhus University
Author for correspondence: Ester Salgarella, esalga@aias.au.dk

Abstract: The Bronze Age Aegean and Cyprus were home to a plethora of scripts, including Cretan Hieroglyphic, Linear A and Linear B, Cypro-Minoan and Cypro-Syllabic. This Element is dedicated to the conventionally named 'Minoan' Linear A script, used on Crete and the Aegean islands during the Middle and Late Bronze Age (ca. 1800–1450 BCE). Linear A is still undeciphered, and the language it encodes ('Minoan') thus remains elusive. Notwithstanding, scholars have been able to extract a good amount of information from Linear A inscriptions and their contexts of use. Current ongoing research, integrating the materiality of script with linguistic analysis, offers a cutting-edge approach with promising results. This Element considers Linear A within an investigative framework as well as narrative, shedding light on a number of burning questions in the field, often the subject of intense academic debate.

Keywords: Aegean Bronze Age, Minoan Linear A, Minoan Crete, Aegean archaeology, Bronze Age Aegean scripts

ISBNs: 9781009520027 (HB), 9781009520065 (PB), 9781009520041 (OC)
ISSNs: 2753-6378 (online), 2753-636X (print)

Contents

1 Defining the (Un)definable: What Is Linear A?   1

2 A Tale of Life and Death: What Is the Lifespan of Linear A?   7

3 The Linear A Corpus: Where Is Linear A Found?   11

4 Drawing Lines: What Does Linear A Look Like?   17

5 Of Clay and Stone (and Else): Where Does Linear A Appear?   22

6 (Beyond) Accounting: What Was Linear A Used For?   26

7 'Elementary, My Dear Watson': What Do We Know from Reading Linear A?   35

8 Speaking in Riddles: Which Language Does Linear A Encode?   46

9 More Unresolved Mysteries: What Do We Not Have in Linear A?   54

10 Current and Future Pathways of Research: What's Next?   58

References   61

An online appendix for this publication and complete list of links to all the inscriptions cited (as published in GORILA online) can be accessed at www.cambridge.org/salgarella

1 Defining the (Un)definable: What Is Linear A?

It is often said that it all starts with the Homeric past.

Does it?

> Κρήτη τις γαῖ' ἔστι μέσῳ ἐνὶ οἴνοπι πόντῳ,
> καλὴ καὶ πίειρα, περίρρυτος· ἐν δ' ἄνθρωποι
> πολλοί, ἀπειρέσιοι, καὶ ἐννήκοντα πόληες.
> ἄλλη δ' ἄλλων γλῶσσα μεμιγμένη· ἐν μὲν Ἀχαιοί,
> ἐν δ' Ἐτεόκρητες μεγαλήτορες, ἐν δὲ Κύδωνες,
> Δωριέες τε τριχάϊκες δῖοί τε Πελασγοί.

> There is a land called Crete, in the midst of the wine-dark sea, a fair, rich land,
> begirt with water, and therein are many men, past counting, and ninety cities.
> They have not all the same speech, but their tongues are mixed. There dwell
> Achaeans, there great-hearted native Cretans, there Cydonians, and Dorians
> of waving plumes, and goodly Pelasgians. (*Odyssey*, book 19: 172ff)[1]

In the *Odyssey*, Crete makes its appearance as multicultural and multilingual. Different peoples are mentioned in what may well be the longest description of Cretan multiculturalism, enriched by linguistic diversity. From this culturally vibrant and myth-infused island, however, no memory seems to have survived of the existence of writing (or a plurality thereof), which by the era of the Greek epics had already been lost to time. We now know that writing did exist in the Aegean way before the archaic period,[2] but partaking in this knowledge is a modern privilege. Where does it all start then? More explicitly for the purposes of our discussion, when was Linear A rediscovered? Before digging up Linear A's past, let us first set out to understand what Linear A *is*.

In mainstream scholarly literature, Linear A is commonly defined as the logo-syllabic, or ideo-syllabic, writing system (or script) used on Crete and the Aegean islands during the Bronze Age (ca. 1800–1450 BCE) to write the still poorly understood Minoan language.[3] Usually, it is also specified that Linear A remains undeciphered to date, despite the many attempts at breaking the code. However accurate, this definition – if read critically – may need some clarification. To begin with, we encounter three terms of common use, whose precise and contextual meaning may not be straightforward: 'writing system', 'script' and 'language'.[4] The first two ('writing system' and 'script') are often used interchangeably, but they refer to different concepts. For the sake of accuracy,

---

[1] Translation courtesy of Perseus Digital Library.

[2] The earliest inscriptions written in the Greek alphabet ('Dipylon inscription', 'Nestor's Cup') date to ca. 740–20 BCE (see esp. Elvira Astoreca 2021).

[3] For a short overview of Linear A, see Salgarella 2022a.

[4] On writing system theory and concepts, see Robinson 2000; Coulmas 2003; Houston 2004; Rogers 2005.

a 'writing system' consists of a 'script', which is the graphic (visual) representation of speech in the form of written signs ('graphemes', from Greek γράφω /gráp^{h}ō/ 'to write'), plus a set of conventions (orthography) that allow a language to be written down correctly.

Here the term 'language' comes into play, making us better understand its role when talking about written communication. Linear A can therefore be referred to as both 'writing system' and 'script', depending on the aspects being studied, but it cannot be addressed as 'language' (too common a mistake in everyday discourse). What Linear A *does* is to write down, as a code, the 'language' spoken by the inhabitants of Bronze Age Crete, the so-called Minoans. Hence we can talk of the 'Minoan language' but not of the 'Linear A language'. This leads us to discuss the term 'undeciphered', equally too often misguidedly used. If we bring to mind that, broadly speaking, 'to decipher' means to convert a code into understandable language, it is therefore accurate to state that Linear A (which is a written code of communication) still remains 'undeciphered', whereas stating that 'Minoan' (which is a language) remains 'undeciphered' is indeed inaccurate.

Let us now move on to less familiar terms: 'logo-syllabic' and 'ideo-syllabic'. These are both used to define a writing system from a typological standpoint and express a variation on the type 'syllabary'. A syllabary (or syllabic writing system) denotes a system in which written characters (commonly called signs) stand for syllables of the coded language, namely units of speech containing a vowel, with or without surrounding consonants (e.g. /a/, /do/, /mi/, etc.). Instead, in alphabetic systems (like English) each character stands for a single sound, be it a vowel or a consonant (e.g. /e/, /m/, /t/). Linear A is understood to be a syllabary, consisting of approximately 150 characters standing for syllables, which are standardly called 'syllabograms' (from Greek γράμμα /grámma/ 'letter'). In addition to syllabograms, Linear A also has a good number of signs (almost 200) understood to represent entire words, concepts or ideas.[5]

If a sign stands for a word, it is called a 'logogram' (from Greek λόγος /lógos/ 'word'). Believe it or not, logograms are also part of our day-to-day life. Think of numbers, for example: characters like '1', '40', '100' stand for entire words in English, since they read as 'one', 'forty', 'one hundred'. Other modern examples are the ampersand ('&'), expected to be read as 'and' (in English, but e.g. 'og' in Danish, 'und' in German, 'e' in Italian and so forth), and the per cent sign '%', read as 'per cent' (in English). If a sign stands for a concept or

---

[5] The conventional list of standardised Linear A signs, still currently used, is given in *GORILA* V: xxii–xxvii.

idea, it is called an 'ideogram' (from Greek ἰδέα /idéa/ 'idea, form'). Are there ideograms in English (and/or other modern languages)? Surprisingly, yes. For example, consider wayfinding signage and street/traffic signs, whose meaning can be understood by people regardless of the language they speak (e.g. arrows indicate directionality). This said, also note that the above examples of 'logograms' in English (i.e. numerals, '&', '%') can be taken as 'ideograms' on a global context, because the ideas (or concepts) they express can be understood regardless of their pronunciation in any given language.

Going back to Linear A, the current consensus is that Linear A may have both logograms and ideograms (with the latter presumably higher in number). Given that Linear A remains undeciphered, a straightforward distinction between these two categories is not easy to make (or may not necessarily need to be made; see especially Salgarella 2020: 42–149). The more-inclusive term 'sematogram' (from Greek σῆμα /sēma/ 'sign') has also been proposed (Petrakis 2012; 2017) to refer to Linear A non-phonetic signs (both 'logograms' and 'ideograms'), which is worth consideration. In this Element, the conventional terminology is retained consistently, since it is widely used in the scholarly literature, with a preference for the more generic term 'ideogram' over 'logogram' (see also Section 4).[6]

Last but not the least, the very name 'Linear A' is not unproblematic: is 'Linear A' the real name of Linear A? Not in the slightest. Most of the terminology used nowadays to refer to the civilisation that flourished in Bronze Age Crete goes back to Sir Arthur Evans (1851–1941), the British archaeologist renowned for unearthing the palace of Knossos on Crete in the early nineteenth century.[7] Not only did he uncover the remains of a civilization whose memory had been lost to time for millennia, but he is also responsible for constructing the narrative surrounding his finds. Drawing on Greek mythology, he dubbed 'Minoans' (after legendary king Minos) the inhabitants of Bronze Age Crete, with Knossos being identified with 'the Palace of Minos'. To Evans we also owe the names 'Cretan Hieroglyphic', 'Linear A' and 'Linear B' to refer to the three Cretan scripts that came to light during his excavations at Knossos. The script understood as the oldest was dubbed 'hieroglyphic' for its pictographic character that reminded Evans of Egyptian hieroglyphs (note that Cretan Hieroglyphic is not derived from Egyptian hieroglyphs, although its creation may have been

---

[6] On the debate surrounding the terminological issue of whether to use 'logogram' or 'ideogram' (or 'sematogram') for the non-phonetic signs of Aegean scripts, see esp. Bennett 1963: 113; Petrakis 2012; Thompson 2012; Melena 2014a: 17, 128–9; Petrakis 2017: 148–51; Palaima 2020: 6, fn. 13.

[7] Evans presented the results of Knossos' excavations in his six-volume monumental work *The Palace of Minos: A Comparative Account of the Successive Stages of the Early Cretan Civilization as Illustrated by the Discoveries at Knossos* (London, 1921–35).

influenced by Egyptian writing).[8] If compared to this earlier script, the two later scripts seemed to Evans more cursive, more 'linear', as it were. Hence the name 'Linear' came about, followed by the letters 'A' and 'B' to distinguish between two slightly different variants as well as chronological stages (Evans' initial dubbing being 'Linear script of Class A' and 'Linear script of Class B').

Linear A was understood to be older than Linear B and also more widespread (with some evidence recently dug up during fieldwork at Haghia Triada in central-south Crete). Linear B, instead, had thus far been found at Knossos only. Since Linear B was not only later in date but also graphically different from Linear A to an extent, Evans initially understood it as a 'calligraphic' variant of Linear A restricted to Knossos. This latter variant, in Evans' view, superseded the former as a result of a dynastic revolution. Later on, Evans changed his mind, seeing Linear A and B as 'parallel' sister scripts derived from 'common prototypes' – these being a sort of proto-linear ancestor whose existence Evans only speculated about but never found evidence of. His views about script relationships, however, changed over time and never quite settled (for a detailed discussion, see Schoep 2018; Salgarella 2020: 10–30). The separation between Linear A and Linear B as different scripts, as well as writing systems, was triggered by the decipherment of Linear B. In 1952 British architect and self-educated linguist Michael Ventris proved that Linear B encoded an early form of the Greek language, subsequently dubbed 'Mycenaean'.[9] Since Linear A could not be decoded in the same way as Linear B, its language remained obscure and most unlikely to be Greek. This linguistic difference brought about a starker cultural separation between Greek-speaking 'Mycenaeans' writing in Linear B and non-Greek-speaking 'Minoans' writing in Linear A. Hence Linear A and Linear B came to be seen as entirely different writing systems and scripts. This view has been influential ever since and has only recently been questioned to promote a more nuanced approach to script development and cultural interpretations (Salgarella 2020).

In the light of the previous discussion, it now becomes clearer why defining 'Linear A' unequivocally is a hard task. For, we have seen that (i) the definition of Linear A as found in print requires further explanation for adequate under-standing; (ii) the name given to this writing system is a modern label and (iii) traditional views on the relationship between Linear A and Linear B may be somewhat misleading, preventing us from reaching a less dichotomous appreciation of their (respective and overall) features. Moreover, we do not have any contemporary sources (e.g. grammatical works, meta-linguistic material; see

---

[8] See esp. Ferrara et al. 2021a.
[9] On Ventris' decipherment, see Chadwick 1967; Pope 2008; Judson 2017; Salgarella 2023.

also Section 9) about what we call 'Linear A', how it worked, how it was created, how it was taught (and transmitted) and its relationship with both (later) Linear B and (earlier) Cretan Hieroglyphic (not to mention Cypro-Minoan, also thought to be an offspring of Linear A). Therefore, when investigating the nature and characteristics of Bronze Age Cretan writing, we resort to using modern approaches, terminology and theoretical frameworks only. There are also other reasons why Linear A defies a clear-cut definition. To better understand these, we first need to contextualise Linear A among the Aegean (and Cypriot) scripts, a few of which readers may be already familiar with. The most well-known are Cretan Hieroglyphic, Linear A, Linear B, Cypro-Minoan and Cypro-Syllabic, while the Arkhanes Script, the scripts of the Phaistos Disk and the Arkalochori Axe, and Eteocretan are perhaps less well-known.[10] Aegean scripts lend themselves to multiple groupings based on the criteria chosen for their classification, as follows.

- *Chronological grouping*: Bronze Age versus Iron Age scripts
  - Bronze Age: Arkhanes Script, Phaistos Disk, Arkalochori Axe, Cretan Hieroglyphic, Linear A, Linear B, Cypro-Minoan
  - Iron Age: Cypro-Syllabic, Eteocretan

- *Geographical grouping*: Cretan versus Cypriot[11]
  - Cretan: Arkhanes Script, Phaistos Disk, Arkalochori Axe, Cretan Hieroglyphic, Linear A, Linear B, Eteocretan
  - Cypriot: Cypro-Minoan, Cypro-Syllabic

- *Typological grouping*: ideo-syllabary versus alphabet
  - Ideo-syllabary: Arkhanes Script, Phaistos Disk, Arkalochori Axe, Cretan Hieroglyphic, Linear A, Linear B, Cypro-Minoan, Cypro-Syllabic
  - Alphabet: Eteocretan (Greek alphabet)

- *Linguistic grouping*: Greek versus non-Greek
  - Greek: Linear B, Cypro-Syllabic
  - Non-Greek: Arkhanes Script, Phaistos Disk, Arkalochori Axe, Cretan Hieroglyphic, Linear A, Cypro-Minoan, Eteocretan

Zooming in on Linear A, it presents itself as a Bronze Age script of Cretan origin, of ideo-syllabic type, encoding a language not yet identified. Having

---

[10] Weilhartner (in press) is the only comprehensive work covering all Aegean scripts. For an overview, see Shelmerdine 2008; Cline 2010; Steele 2023.

[11] This opposition is not strict, since inscriptions belonging to either category are also found in Crete's and Cyprus' respective areas of influence (for Cretan scripts, the Aegean islands, perhaps the Levant; for Cypriot scripts, the Aegean islands and Ugarit).

placed Linear A in a broader context, we can now mention another reason why it defies a clear-cut definition. This is the graphic similarity Linear A shows with a number of Aegean scripts, which makes it difficult to draw straight lines between categories. Looking backward in time, the origins of Linear A have blurred boundaries: among the earliest Linear A inscriptions, there are a few labelled *dubitanda* (i.e. 'of doubtful reading'), as they could equally be taken as written in Cretan Hieroglyphic (listed in *CHIC*: 18); likewise, the Arkhanes Script is taken as either an early form (or ancestor) of Linear A or a separate (yet related) script.[12] Needless to say, the debate surrounding the relations between Linear A, the Phaistos Disk and Arkalochori Axe is also far from settled.

Looking forward in time, we find Linear A's offspring Linear B. We have seen that Evans' understanding of Linear A and Linear B as either one or two scripts fluctuated over time, without ever truly settling. The split between Linear A and Linear B as different scripts (the former associated with the 'Minoans', the latter with the 'Mycenaeans') became sharper after the decipherment of Linear B, when script designations came to take on cultural meaning.[13] This view has influenced subsequent approaches to script development as well as our appreciation of the population groups we currently dub 'Minoans' and 'Mycenaeans'. Scholars are now distancing themselves from dichotomous classifications, in favour of a more nuanced and fluid approach emphasising the role played by progressive, incremental change in both script development and cultural transformation, as well as problematising implicit associations of material culture (of which 'script' is part) with broader, blanket-like cultural narratives.[14]

Dismissing the role of progressive change may, in fact, have been a contributing factor to a contrastive distinction between Linear A and Linear B. There is a real chronological gap of about fifty years between the latest (extant) inscriptions in Linear A and the earliest (extant) inscriptions in Linear B. It is unclear whether this absence of written evidence from the archaeological record reflects a real historical circumstance or it is simply due to chance and accidents of preservation. Until further evidence is discovered (if ever), there is no way of proving (or disproving) either hypothesis. At the current state of knowledge, this absence implies that we do not know what the Linear script may have looked like

---

[12] On the nature of the Arkhanes Script (or 'formula') and its relations with the other Cretan scripts, see esp. Decorte 2018a; Ferrara et al. 2021b (with further references).

[13] See esp. Salgarella 2020: 10–32. On the term 'Minoan' before Evans, see Karadimas and Momigliano 2004.

[14] See e.g. Bennet 1999; Bennet 2002: 221; Hamilakis 2002; Driessen and Langohr 2007; Galanakis 2015; Salgarella 2020: 10–32; Galanakis 2022.

in the transitional period from the so-called Minoan to Mycenaean administration on Crete.

To conclude, what we dub 'Linear A' is a tricky entity that needs to be handled with intellectual care. General, broadly applied definitions fail to describe what still escapes our full understanding, for which there are more questions than answers. This Element, therefore, aims to problematise what we know about 'Linear A' by raising a set of (still hotly debated) questions and by offering to readers the most comprehensive and research-informed array of plausible hypotheses put forward to date in the academic debate.

2 A Tale of Life and Death: What Is the Lifespan of Linear A?

Surely not a short-lived script, Linear A's life spanned nearly five centuries from ca. 1800 to 1450 BCE.[15] In scholarly literature, we also find the alternative nomenclature 'from Middle Minoan II to Late Minoan IB', with reference to relative dating. Relative dating may not be as straightforward as absolute dating (which provides specific dates), because relative dating creates chronological sequences that give an estimate of how old an artefact is in comparison to other artefacts and/or archaeological sites, without however specifying its absolute age. Since pottery is often used as a diagnostic tool to determine the relative order of sequences, we often call these 'pottery phases'. In addition to 'pottery phases', we can also find labels referring to geographically-based 'cultural phases', following a culture-historical approach to archaeological dating. Hence the absolute dates 1800 to 1450 BCE correspond to 'Proto-Palatial' ('First Palaces') to 'Neo-Palatial' ('New Palaces') periods on Crete (Table 1).

Most Linear A evidence comes from Late Minoan IB, corresponding to the end of the Neo-Palatial period (ca. 1450 BCE). This period was characterised by island-wide, large-scale destructive events, during which almost all Minoan palatial centres ('palaces') were destroyed. A seismic island, Crete was most likely hit by severe earthquakes followed by fires, which, on the bright side, were responsible for baking Linear A inscriptions on clay and thus preserving them until today. Indeed, most Linear A evidence that has come down to us consists of small clay tablets used as administrative records for the bookkeeping of palatial centres, although other materials (e.g. stone) were also used as writing media (on material supports, see Section 5; on document types, see Section 6). The destruction that took place around 1450 BCE marked the end of the Neo-Palatial period, argued to coincide with the

---

[15] After Salgarella 2020: 42–6, with further references about Bronze Age Aegean chronologies. See also Schoep 1995; Schoep 2002: 17–21; Decorte 2018b.

Table 1 Absolute and relative dating of Linear A[16]

Absolute dating (high)	Pottery phase	Cultural phase	Scripts in use
1900–1800	Middle Minoan II	Proto-Palatial	Cretan Hieroglyphic and Linear A
1800–1700	Middle Minoan III		
1700–1600	Late Minoan IA	Neo-Palatial	Linear A
1600–1450	Late Minoan IB		
1450–1400	Late Minoan II	Final-Palatial	(?)
1400–1375	Late Minoan III A1		Linear B
1375–1300	Late Minoan III A2	Post-Palatial	Linear B
1300–1200	Late Minoan III B		

end of the 'Minoan' civilisation as well (although softer approaches are being explored). After this event Linear A ceased to be used, at least in administrative contexts, due to the fall of the system for whose purposes Linear A was mostly employed (and perhaps created?). No written documents survive from the following period (Late Minoan II). We need to wait until Late Minoan III (ca. 1400–1375 BCE) to witness the earliest (extant) evidence of Linear B.

Although the most severe, the 1450 BCE destruction was not the only one. The ends of the other period 'breaks' (as illustrated in Table 1) are equally characterised by destruction horizons. Thanks to these destructions and changes in material culture, archaeologists theorise successive chronological blocks, characterised by some degree of internal uniformity.[17] This is why the chronologies illustrated in Table 1 appear that way. Unfortunate as these events were for causing serious physical damage, they are also the fortunate reason behind the preservation of Linear A clay administrative records throughout time, until today (see Section 6.1). It has to be borne in mind that most of the extant evidence has therefore survived because of accidents of preservation, meaning that we do not have the whole picture of Linear A use (see Section 9 on the likely existence of written documents in perishable

---

[16] Adapted from Salgarella 2020, table 1. Absolute dating after Warren and Hankey 1989.
[17] On the implications of the 'block-time' approach (Proto-, Pre-, Neo-, Final-, Post-Palatial) for the reconstruction of major cultural developments in Minoan society (including script and administrative systems), see Schoep's forthcoming work on the subject.

materials, such as parchment and/or papyrus, obliterated by fire destructions). Whenever a centre (palatial or not)[18] was destroyed, it provided us with a snapshot of contemporary Linear A use. Although the bulk of Linear A is dated to Late Minoan IB (especially evidence from Haghia Triada and Khania), some sites underwent slightly earlier destructions (Phaistos: Middle Minoan IIB–IIIB; Mallia: Middle Minoan IIIB; Knossos, Akrotiri: Late Minoan IA) or later (Zakros: very end of Late Minoan IB; geography discussed in Section 3).

So, when do we find the earliest evidence of Linear A? This is not uncontroversial and is inextricably intertwined with theories on the 'birth' of Linear A, calling into question its relation with two earlier Cretan scripts (Cretan Hieroglyphic and the Arkhanes Script).[19] The earliest known inscriptions argued to be written in Linear A date to Middle Minoan II (ca. 1900–1800 BCE)[20] and have blurred boundaries with Cretan Hieroglyphic. The Middle Minoan period, in fact, saw the rise and fall of Cretan Hieroglyphic, with its archival documents spanning Middle Minoan II (Knossos, Petras) to III (Mallia). A few clay inscriptions found at Knossos and Mallia, currently published in the corpus of Cretan Hieroglyphic (*CHIC*: 18), may however be equally taken as Linear A and are hence labelled *dubitanda* ('of doubtful reading').

Is this circumstance suggestive of a derivation of Linear A from Cretan Hieroglyphic? Maybe – or maybe not. The problem is that evidence for both scripts appear as early as Middle Minoan II, with Cretan Hieroglyphic taking flight first, especially on north Crete (Knossos, Mallia, Petras), whereas Linear A comes second, spreading from central-south Crete (Phaistos). If Cretan Hieroglyphic had the edge over Linear A in the Middle Minoan period, Linear A clearly lorded it over the former in Late Minoan I. But which one was first invented then? Perhaps thinking in terms of chronological precedence is not a productive way of addressing this issue. It has recently been suggested that, instead of theorising script development in monogenetic, unidirectional evolutionary terms (with one system developing straight out of another), the emergence of writing on Crete may be best understood as a sequence of step-like inventions, 'as rapid bursts followed by subsequent modifications that extended over long

---

[18] It is worth pointing out that although the majority of Linear A administrative documents come from 'palatial' centres, some evidence also comes from extra-palatial contexts (e.g. Myrtos Pyrgos).

[19] On graphic relations between Cretan Hieroglyphic and the other Cretan scripts, see lastly Meissner and Salgarella 2024 (with further references). On processes of script-sign creation, see lastly Salgarella 2021 (with further references).

[20] This includes a tablet fragment from Knossos (KN 49, published in Macdonald and Knappett 2007, pl. 46) and a painted larnax rim from Arkhanes (ARKH Zc 8, published in Sakellarakis and Sapouna-Sakellaraki 1997) (see Decorte 2018b: 22–3 for further references).

periods of time' (Schoep 2020: 52).[21] The inspiration for the formation of full-fledged writing systems in Middle Minoan may be found in earlier experimentations with writing which took place in the previous period, namely Early Minoan sealstones and the Arkhanes Script.[22] However, as of now, there is no probative evidence for these to be taken as early forms of either Cretan Hieroglyphic or Linear A. The precise dynamics behind the emergence of writing on Crete, complex as they are, still elude us and are a subject of academic inquiry.

Let us now move to the opposite side of the timeline: what is the latest datable evidence of Linear A? As mentioned, Linear A did not outlast the fall of the (Neo-)Palatial system at the end of Late Minoan IB.[23] In the following period (Late Minoan II), we witness what is often called an 'epigraphic gap', without evidence of writing. Yet this is not entirely true. In fact, if writing seems not to have survived the 1450 BCE destruction horizon outside of 'formal' contexts (i.e. palatial structures or places for cultic activity), there is some evidence suggesting that writing had not been entirely lost. We have a few Linear A spillovers from 'informal' contexts, all coming (most notably) from the area around Knossos: two carved inscriptions (Late Minoan II), one on a building block, the other on a pithoid jar; two painted inscriptions (Late Minoan IIIA1), one on a cultic figurine, the other on a miniature cup.[24]

This epigraphic silence was broken around 1400 to 1375 BCE, which produced the earliest Linear B inscriptions known to date.[25] Linear B appears like a burst, as much a full-fledged writing system as Linear A was. But how so, given the preceding epigraphic gap? It is still unclear whether absence of evidence (from Late Minoan II) is actual evidence of absence or rather a chance event due to accidents of preservation. Yet, this absence prevents us from appreciating how Linear B originated (and when exactly) or, better, from understanding how this 'Linear Script' gradually developed over time transitioning from Linear A (accommodating the Minoan language) to Linear B (accommodating the Greek language). This transition, as well as transformation, has been variously explored by scholars to better understand the

---

[21] On Linear A's early beginnings, see also Ferrara 2015; Decorte 2018b.

[22] Argued to be the earliest evidence of Cretan writing, the Arkhanes Script (ca. 2100–1800 BCE) only occurs on fourteen sealstones as a formulaic inscription (Arkhanes Formula). See esp. Decorte 2018a; Ferrara et al., 2021b.

[23] On the 'end' of Linear A, see esp. Bennet 2008.

[24] Building block from the Kephala tomb (KN Ze 16, *GORILA* IV: 138); pithoid jar from Knossos' Unexplored Mansion (KN Zb 40, *GORILA* IV: 83); figurine from Poros (PO Zc 1, published in Dimopoulou et al. 1993); miniature cup from Khania (KH Zc 106, published in Hallager and Hallager 2016: 290–2), imported from Knossos. See Salgarella 2020: 43 for further references.

[25] From the *Room of the Chariot Tablets* at Knossos (Driessen 2000).

dynamics at play in the close context of the Linear Script's transmission.[26] The traditional view splitting Linear A and Linear B into two different units strictly associated with their respective 'culture' (Cretan Minoans versus Mainlander Mycenaeans) is now being revised in favour of a more fluid approach to both script development and societal change. The Linear Script may have survived through time, gradually adapting some of its components to suit changing needs and accommodate new features (e.g. language, purposes, uses). Ultimately, it may well not have been the end of Linear A. Linear A may never have 'died', as much as Linear B may never have been 'born': the latter may be seen as the gradual transformation of the former, captured by us in a later chronological snapshot, under different conditions of use. Seen this way, the 'Linear' line was never truly broken.

3 The Linear A Corpus: Where Is Linear A Found?

A total of fifty-six sites ('findplaces') have so far yielded Linear A inscriptions. Most findplaces are located on Crete and the Aegean islands, but a few sites located in Mainland Greece, Western Anatolia and the Levant also yielded some evidence. On Crete, the most evidence comes from Haghia Triada, Khania and Zakros, all dated to the destruction horizon that brought to an end the Neo-Palatial period (Late Minoan IB). Other relevant findplaces are Phaistos, Knossos, Mallia, Arkhanes, Tylissos and Palaikastro. In the Aegean islands, inscriptions have been found in Thera, Kythera, Kea, Melos and Samothrace. The evidence from outside of Crete is sparse, fragmentary and often of doubtful reading. In Mainland Greece finds come from Haghios Stephanos, Argos and Mycenae. In Western Anatolia Miletus and possibly Troy have yielded some evidence, and in Israel inscriptions have been dug out at Tel Haror and Tel Lachish (Figures 1–2).[27] Most Linear A inscriptions were found in 'administrative' contexts, functioning as records of economic transactions for the book-keeping of palatial administrations, but a smaller number of inscriptions also come from 'non-administrative' contexts with a cultic and/or dedica-tory function (see Section 6).

---

[26] Lastly Salgarella 2019; Salgarella 2020 (with further references).

[27] For an overview of the geographical distribution of Linear A see Salgarella 2020: 2–4, 42–9; Schoep 2002: 17–22. Most documents from Crete, Mainland Greece and the Aegean islands are published in *GORILA*. For those from outside Crete not included there, see Palaima 2003 (Mycenae); Protonotariou-Deilaki 1990 (Mycenae, Argos); Taylour and Janko 2008: 441–3 (Haghios Stephanos, also in *GORILA* V: 16); Niemeier 1996 (Miletus); Brown 1997 (Troy); Oren 1996 (Tel Haror); Finkelberg et al. 1996: 195–207 (Tel Lachish).

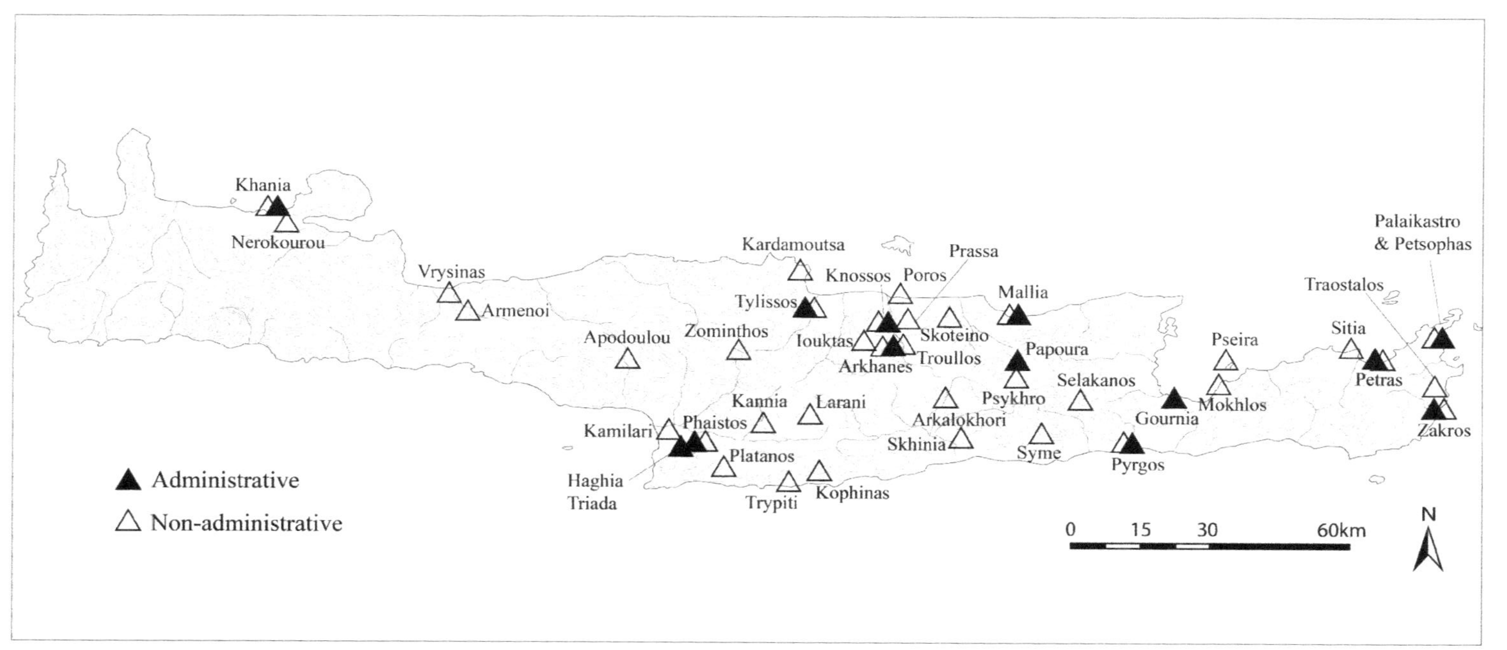

Figure 1 Main findplaces of Linear A inscriptions: Crete.[28]

---

[28] After Salgarella 2020: 2.

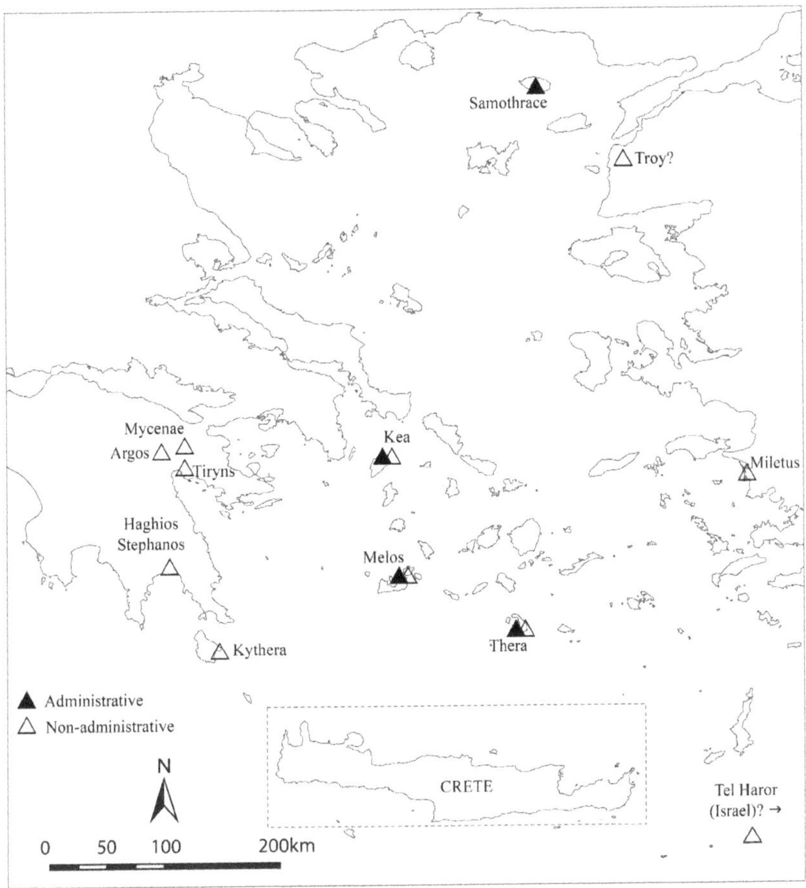

Figure 2 Main findplaces of Linear A inscriptions: outside of Crete.[29]

Now that we have seen where Linear A inscriptions come from, let us have a look at how much is extant: how much Linear A evidence do we have to date? All in all, the corpus of Linear A inscriptions is relatively small. Statistically speaking, only approximately 1,400 inscriptions are preserved well enough to be readable (Schoep 2002: 38), out of a total of around 2,500 finds (including fragmentary evidence). If we had to count every individual sign occurrence in these inscriptions, we would reach an estimated total of 7,400 (Schoep 2002: 38), meaning that 'if there are 4002 characters (font Times New Roman, pitch 12, no spaces) on a 8 1/2 × 11 inch sheet of paper with 1-inch margins, all extant Linear A would take up 1.84 pages'.[30] Aside

---

[29] After Salgarella 2020: 3.
[30] Younger 2024 (*Linear A Texts: Introduction*, section 4, 'Basic Statistics').

from the small size of the corpus, what complicates the picture is that Linear A inscriptions are also relatively short, and the longest ones are formulaic (i.e. consisting of repeated groups of words). As a result, Linear A inscriptions display very limited syntax, which makes it difficult to investigate the language in which they are written (discussed in Section 7). So, 'what' from 'where' then? The total amount of Linear A evidence so far unearthed is given in Table 2, where references are made to both (i) each individual site that has produced inscriptions (alphabetical order) and (ii) whether the inscriptions found come from an administrative context (palatial setting) or not (mostly cultic/ritual). This is the traditional classification of Linear A inscriptions, based on the 'function' they are understood to have fulfilled (see Sections 5 and 6).

Table 2 Findplaces (with standard abbreviations) of Linear A, with the amount of evidence yielded[31]

Site	Non-administrative	Administrative	Total
Apodoulou (AP)	3	–	3
Argos (ARG)	1	–	1
Arkalokhori (AR)	2	–	2
Arkhanes (ARKH)	2	7	9
Armenoi (ARM)	1	–	1
Crete (CR)	4	–	4
Gournia (GO)	–	3	3
Haghia Triada (HT)	19	1,250	1,269
Haghios Stephanos (HS)	1	–	1
Iouktas (IO)	16	–	16
Kamilari (KAM)	1	–	1
Kannia (KAN)	1	–	1
Kardamoutsa (KA)	1	–	1
Kea (KE)	5	2	7
Khania (KH)	1	312	313
Knossos (KN)	24	8	32
Kophinas (KO)	2	–	2
Kythera (KY)	2	–	2

---

[31] Based on Schoep 2002: 15–16, 20–1, and Younger 2024 (*Linear A Texts in Phonetic Transcription: Haghia Triada; Linear A Texts in Phonetic Transcription: Other Texts*). Younger updated his website until April 2024, which includes all Linear A inscriptions published until then (esp. after *GORILA* V).

Table 2 (cont.)

Site	Non-administrative	Administrative	Total
Larani (LA)	1	–	1
Mallia (MA)	3	8	11
Melos (MI)	2	1	3
Miletus (MIL)	1	–	1
Mokhlos (MO)	3	–	3
Mycenae (MY)	2	–	2
Nerokourou (NE)	1	–	1
Palaikastro (PK)	21	2	23
Papoura (PA)	–	1	1
Petras (PE)	7	3	10
Petsofas (PETS)	–	1	1
Phaistos (PH)	4	61	65
Platanos (PL)	1	–	1
Poros (PO)	1	–	1
Prassas (PR)	1	–	1
Pseira (PSI)	2	–	2
Psychro (PS)	1	–	1
Pyrgos (PYR)	1	3	4
Samothrace (SAM)	–	2	2
Selakanos (SE)	1	–	1
Sitia (SI)	1	–	1
Skinia (SK)	1	–	1
Skoteino (SK)	1	–	1
Syme (SY)	12	–	12
Tel Haror (TEL)	1	–	1
Tel Lachish (LACH)	1	–	1
Thera (THE)	8	6	14
Tiryns (TI)	1	–	1
Traostalos (TRA)	1	–	1
Troullos (TL)	1	–	1
Troy (TRO)	2	–	2
Trypiti (TRY)	1	–	1
Tylissos (TY)	2	3	5
Vrysinas (VRY)	1	–	1
Zakros (ZA)	4	591	595
Zominthos (ZO)	1	–	1
Total	**178**	**2,265**	**2,443**

Last but not least, where is this evidence stored? And, more interesting for the reader, where can *we* see this material? The answer is an easy one: museums. Most of the Linear A evidence is stored in Greek museums (especially Cretan), although a few inscriptions are also on display elsewhere. Let us start with Greece. The bulk of the material dug out on Crete is on display at the Archaeological Museum of Heraklion, followed by the Archaeological Museums of Khania, Petras/Siteia and Haghios Nikolaos. In the Aegean islands, some Linear A is at the Archaeological Museums of Thera (Santorini), Kythera and Kea. In Mainland Greece, evidence is on display at the National Archaeological Museum of Athens, the Archaeological Museum of Mesara and the Piraeus Museum. Outside Greece, a few inscriptions can be found at the Museo Pigorini (Rome) and at the Ashmolean Museum (Oxford).[32]

However, it is not necessary to travel long distances to see some Linear A. In the contemporary digital age, effort is being put into making digital collections available online, although we are still at the very outset of this undertaking (a list of currently available resources is given in Section 10). Digital projects aside, the two standard scientific editions of Linear A inscriptions are Raison and Pope's (1994) *Corpus transnuméré du linéaire A* and Godart and Olivier's (1976–85) *Recueil des inscriptions en Linéaire A*, in five volumes (known as *GORILA*, with scans available online at http://cefael.efa.gr/result.php?site_id=1&serie_id=EtCret, *Études crétoises*, 21). Although the latter is now the most widely perused for its photographic set, the former is still valuable in providing detailed archaeological and bibliographical references. A few discrepancies aside, the two editions mostly differ in their respective numbering system of Linear A signs. The five volumes of *GORILA* contain all Linear A evidence published until 1976. Later finds are published in a Supplement (GORILA Supplement 1, Del Freo and Zurbach 2025; announced in Del Freo and Zurbach 2011), with a few finds already published in specialist journals.

Unlike the aforementioned digital projects, *GORILA* is aimed at a specialist audience only and is not (strictly speaking) user-friendly. For every inscription, a black-and-white photograph is given, alongside a drawing and a transcription of the Linear A signs it shows in their 'standardised/ normalised' shape. However, no phonetic transcription is given, meaning that inscriptions cannot be 'read' in a phonetic fashion. But we shall not despair: on his Academia.edu collected papers (from the former website

---

[32] Special thanks go to Dr Georgia Flouda for confirming this list.

Linear A Texts in Phonetic Transcription & Commentary, https://bit.ly/
4c4fSLo, University of Kansas), John Younger (Emeritus Professor) provides a phonetic reading of inscriptions by applying to Linear A signs the
conventional phonetic values of their corresponding Linear B signs. By
moving back and forth between *GORILA* (visual information) and
Younger's transcriptions (textual information), we can come up with
a good overview (and reading) of the extant Linear A evidence (see
Section 7). A new digital, interactive and updatable edition of the corpus
is a *desideratum* in the field. It is hoped this wish will soon be granted to
benefit specialists and general readership alike.

4 Drawing Lines: What Does Linear A Look Like?

Straight, curved, segmented, dotted – Linear A is composed of various 'lines'
(Figure 3). When combined together, lines form 'signs', the basic graphic units
of a script. The standard list of Linear A signs (*GORILA* V: xxii–xxvii) shows
a total of 390 signs. Yet these signs are not all of the same type. These can be
classified based on either form or function: if the former, we end up having
'simple' versus 'complex' signs; if the latter, we have 'syllabograms' versus
'ideograms' (on terminology, see Section 1). Scripts are, in fact, very much like
coins, showing two different yet inextricably linked sides: one side representing

Figure 3 What a Linear A inscription looks like (ZA 10a, *GORILA* III: 168).[33]

---

[33] Drawing by Salgarella.

their graphic (visual) 'form', the other their 'function'. When talking about 'form', we mean what the script (and its signs) looks like on a visual level (sign shapes, ductus, etc.), whereas 'function' refers to the function performed by signs to convey a specific type of information (e.g. phonetic, ideographic, numerical, structural, etc.).

We have seen (in Section 1) that Linear A has both phonetic and non-phonetic components: roughly 150 syllabograms (phonetic signs) and almost 200 ideograms (non-phonetic signs, standing for words or concepts). This way, signs are classified following a functional approach (which is the one adopted for Linear B sign classification). Alongside syllabograms and ideograms, there are just under fifty signs ('klasmatograms') representing mathematical values (not speech), more specifically fractions (*GORILA* V: xxvii). At times, signs occur in isolation (i.e. they are neither part of a word nor ideograms), often placed within dots: these are called 'isolated signs', which are standardly subdivided into the categories of 'transaction signs' and 'simple signs' (more on this in what follows). There are also signs for numerical units (although not included in the standard sign list): a short vertical stroke represents one unit, a short horizontal stroke is a ten, a circle is one hundred. Finally, Linear A seems to have one punctuation mark, which comes in the shape of a small dot (not consistently used in inscriptions) and isolated signs (Figure 4).

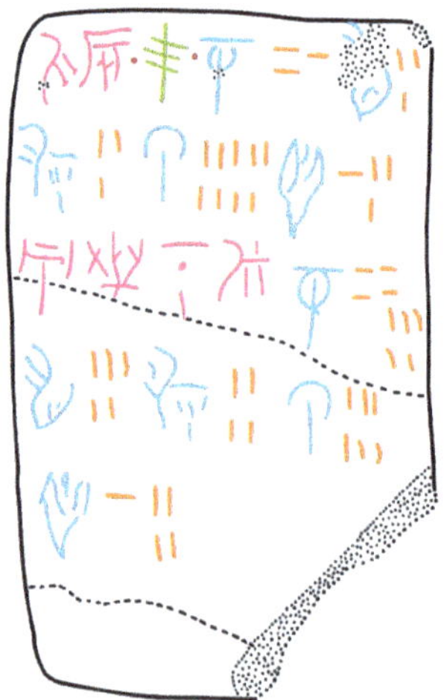

Figure 4 Functional classification of Linear A signs (HT 14, *GORILA* I: 28–9): syllabograms (pink), ideograms (blue), transaction sign (green), numbers (orange), punctuation marks (red).[34]

---

[34] Drawing by Salgarella.

This functional approach to Linear A sign classification (much influenced by Linear B sign classification) is coupled with a formal approach. In fact, *GORILA*'s standard sign list does not group signs based on whether they function as either syllabograms or ideograms (which is at times a controversial choice to make) but rather groups them based on their graphic form: 'simple' versus 'complex'. However useful, this double approach to Linear A sign classification may turn out to be slightly confusing. 'Form' and 'function' are so deeply intertwined that even in standard scholarship there is no single way of classifying Linear A signs (see the discussion in Salgarella 2020: 42–149; Salgarella 2022b). Let us look at these two aspects one by one to get a better understanding of what Linear A *looks like* and how it *functions*.

On a graphic level, signs are either 'simple', meaning they consist of one single graphic unit, or 'complex' (or 'composite'), meaning they are a combination of two or more simple signs (thus being a complex graphic unit). Based on how simple signs are combined together, we can have different types of complex signs: 'ligatured' complex signs result from fusing together two or more simple signs (sharing a number of traits, e.g. A 559 in Figure 5), while 'juxtaposed' complex signs are formed by simply juxtaposing two simple signs (e.g. A 608 in Figure 5). Sometimes it is unquestionably challenging (or not possible at all) to assign a complex sign to either of these two categories, as

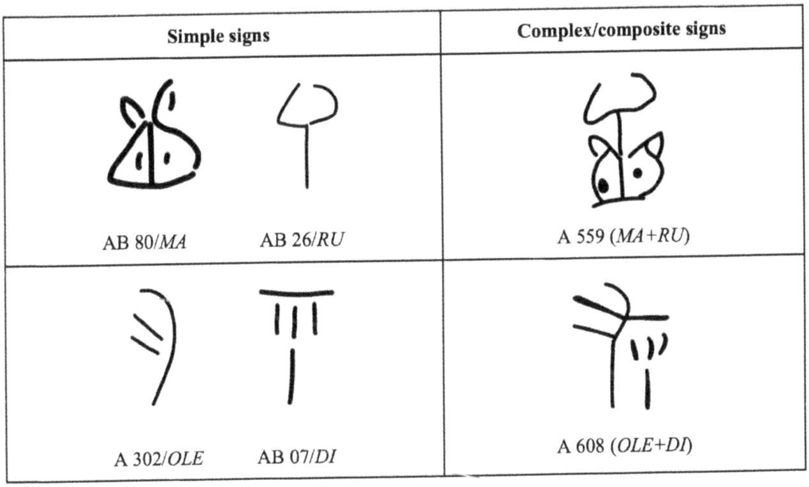

Simple signs		Complex/composite signs
AB 80/*MA*	AB 26/*RU*	A 559 (*MA+RU*)
A 302/*OLE*	AB 07/*DI*	A 608 (*OLE+DI*)

Figure 5 Formal classification of Linear A signs: 'simple' versus 'complex/composite'.[35]

---

[35] Drawings by Salgarella.

it could equally fit in both. Let us not forget that these classifications are modern conventions: we do not know how Bronze Age writers conceptualised Linear A signs (see also Section 9.3). These classifications are just ways for us to make sense of something whose underlying principles we do not yet fully understand. We shall thus never forget that the applicability and effectiveness of this taxonomy has its own limitations.

Sometimes complex signs represent 'monograms', whose individual components spell out a word. Wait, how do we know this if Linear A is undeciphered? We know this thanks to a very fortunate piece of evidence allowing us to read and translate a Linear A monogram. This is complex sign A 559, reading (bottom-up) as *MA+RU*, if signs are given the phonetic values of their Linear B counterparts (on Linear A 'readability', see Section 7). This word is thought to be the term for 'wool' in Minoan. In fact, not only was this complex sign retained in Linear B and used as the ideogram for wool (Linear B sign *145/*LANA*), but also the term *maru* is likely to have been borrowed into Greek as μαλλός /mallós/ 'wool/fleece'.[36] Do we have more such examples? Not quite. Whether more (or most/all?) Linear A ligatured signs may represent words (and therefore be given a phonetic reading) is still unclear.

It is now time to become more familiar with the standard sign list in order to understand how to 'find' a Linear A sign and how to cite it in writing. In *GORILA*'s sign list, signs appear in order of increasing graphic complexity: first come simple signs ('signes simples', *GORILA* V: xxii–xxiii), then complex signs ('signes complexes', *GORILA* V: xxiv–xxvii), followed by all attested combinations of fractional signs ('fractions simples et complexes', *GORILA* V: xxvii).[37] Each sign is given a number in ascending order (starting from 01), preceded by a prefix: 'A' if the sign is only attested in Linear A, while 'AB' if the sign is shared with Linear B (note that not all Linear A signs were continued onto Linear B). In this latter case, it is often thought that the shared sign ('homomorph') had a comparable phonetic reading ('homophone') in Linear A. Given that the phonetic values of Linear B are known, it is quite common to supply an approximate phonetic reading to an 'AB' sign in Linear A, alongside its classification number. Hence, here is what a Linear A sign's ID looks like: AB 01/*DA* (AB sign, with approximate phonetic

---

[36] The Greek word for 'wool' is λῆνος /lēnos/. The term μαλλός /mallós/ 'fleece' is still found in Hesiod (*Works and Days*, 234). Hesychius attests the gloss 'μάλλυκες : τρίχες', meaning that /màllukes/ is a Cretan word translatable as /trik^hes/ 'hair'.

[37] For (approximate) values of Linear A klasmatograms (fractional signs), see Younger 2024 (*Linear A Texts: Introduction*, section 14, 'Fractions,' and section 15, 'Metrology').

reading given, i.e. /da/), A 301 (Linear A–only sign). In case a sign also behaves as an ideogram, whose meaning is known from its Linear B counterpart, the Latin name of the commodity the sign stands for is also given (following Linear B conventional nomenclature):[38] for example, 'AB 21 *QI/OVIS*', where *OVIS* is the Latin word for 'sheep', meaning that the sign is also used as the 'sheep' ideogram. In case of animal ideograms, the gendered version is specified with a superscript: for example, *OVIS^f* 'female sheep' (ewe) versus *OVIS^m* 'male sheep' (ram). The complete list of Linear A signs (alongside the ideograms' Latin names) is given in the supplementary online appendix (provided in the Contents section at the beginning of this Element).

Moving onto 'function', we have seen that a functional classification groups signs based on which function they perform in an inscription (or text, more generically): syllabograms perform a phonetic function, ideograms stand for ideas or concepts, klasmatograms represent mathematical values. On top of these, sometimes Linear A inscriptions show isolated signs, whose function is not straightforwardly identifiable with any of the above. So, how do we determine which function a sign performs? Mostly by context. In fact, it is not possible simply to guess at a sign's function based on its graphic/formal appearance only: simple signs may behave both as syllabograms and ideograms (despite statistically showing a preference for the former); composite signs prefer an ideographic behaviour, yet we have seen that 'monograms' spell out words and therefore can be read phonetically.

To determine which function a sign performs with more certainty, we look at where it appears: if a sign is part of a sign-sequence and is therefore used to write what we assume is a word (this is not always obvious in Linear A), it behaves as a syllabogram; if a sign occurs alone after clearly identifiable sign-sequences (mostly at the end of an entry), it behaves as an ideogram. Isolated signs are identifiable by way of exclusion, as they do not belong in either of the previously mentioned contexts: as their name tells, they are 'isolated', associable with neither a precise sign-sequence nor an ideogram.[39] At times isolated signs are placed between dots (the Linear A 'punctuation' mark), as if to indicate to readers, by standing out from the rest of the text, that they refer to 'something else' (see the black dots on the first line of Figure 4). The problem is that we do not know what exactly this 'something else' is. It has been

---

[38] The most comprehensive and recent work on Linear B is Killen 2024a (with the most up-to-date conventional sign list).

[39] Salgarella (2020: 52–4, 299, 372) argues that 'isolated signs' may perform a supra-structural function and be taken as stand-alone signs.

suggested (Schoep 2002: 37–9, 135–43) that isolated signs may sometimes refer to the type or nature of the transaction recorded in the inscription (as most Linear A texts are administrative records; see Section 6); in such cases, they are called 'transaction signs' (see Section 8.2).

In sum, we have seen that neither a fully formal nor a fully functional classification is a productive way of classifying Linear A signs. Both classifications are in fact needed and useful based on which specific aspect of the script we want to focus on and explore. Both 'form' and 'function' always need to be borne in mind, given their inextricable intertwining. However challenging studying Linear A may be, we shall refrain from 'flipping a coin' when undecided: let us always take into account both sides of the 'Linear A coin', making them interchange in a productive way.

5 Of Clay and Stone (and Else): Where Does Linear A Appear?

This section focuses on the materiality of the Linear A script (see esp. Flouda 2013, 2015). What do we mean by 'materiality' in this context? A wide-ranging term, 'materiality' refers to the materials (e.g. clay, stone) used to shape the objects meant to accommodate writing (standardly called writing 'supports' or 'media'), as well as the implements used to write inscriptions (e.g. brush, stylus).[40] Based on the medium and implement chosen, which provide material *affordances* and *constraints* (see e.g. Salgarella in press), different techniques can be adopted to write inscriptions. As a modern example, let us take writing on paper (medium): with a pen (implement), the technique is inking; with a pencil, it is drawing; with a brush, it is painting. The same applies to Linear A: on the same medium (clay), an inscription can be incised (with a stylus), painted (with a brush), or carved (with carving tools). In Aegean scholarship, inscriptions are often referred to as 'written documents', which can be classified based on function and typology (see Section 6).

In the Linear A context, the material aspects of an inscription and the function it performs very often go hand in hand and are deeply intertwined, although there is no strict one-to-one correspondence between writing medium and function (see Section 6). For instance, clay is the preferred medium for administrative inscriptions (e.g. records of economic transactions), but it can also be used to accommodate inscriptions fulfilling other purposes (e.g. cultic, ritual, dedicatory). So, how much material diversity is there in Linear A? We could say

---

[40] The theoretical framework called 'materiality of writing' for the study of ancient scripts and inscriptions is put forward by Piquette and Whitehouse (2013).

that Linear A inscriptions show reasonably broad material diversity, if compared to the other full-fledged Bronze Age Aegean scripts (i.e. Cretan Hieroglyphic, Linear B, Cypro-Minoan). However, Linear A inscriptions are much less diverse if compared to other ancient contexts (e.g. Egypt, the Near East). Therefore, also in this case (as often when discussing Linear A), answering this question is a matter of perspective.

Now, we may wonder whether the extant material diversity (presented in the following sections) is representative of the overall Linear A production or if it is just a snapshot of what might have existed and is forever lost to us: is this a real or an apparent 'richness'? In other words, is it that not much has survived to us or that not much was produced? This is hard to evaluate on present evidence. Overall, Linear A does not appear to have been widely employed (as much as we use 'writing' nowadays, or if compared to nearby contemporary contexts such as Egypt and the Near East), since the extant Linear A evidence comes from a number of specific contexts only (administrative or cultic). The function of Linear A 'written documents' is the subject of Section 6, while Section 9 is dedicated to 'what is missing' (and 'what we may expect') from the archaeological record.

In what follows, an illustration is given of the material supports/media of Linear A inscriptions, their writing implements and writing techniques, which will set the foundations for discussing document typology and function in Section 6.

5.1 Materials

Based on extant evidence, the materials used to produce Linear A inscriptions are as follows:

- Clay: either accidentally or intentionally baked (see Section 6.1)
- Stone (hard and soft): mostly steatite, serpentine, limestone; more rarely marble, alabaster, chlorite, schist (see Sections 6.2.1, 6.2.4 and 6.2.5)
- Metal: gold, silver, bronze, perhaps copper (see Section 6.2.2)
- Bone: ivory, hippopotamus tusks (see Section 6.2.5)
- Plaster (see Section 6.2.3)

5.2 Writing media

5.2.1 Supports

A great variety of writing media (i.e. objects receiving writing) were produced to accommodate Linear A texts. The most common writing media are made out of clay, to such an extent that the Linear A writing practice may be argued to follow a *clay+* trend. Clay was shaped into different objects ('document types', most notably tablets and sealings; see Section 6) with one or more surfaces to accommodate writing. No wonder why clay was chosen as a preferential material: clay is abundant on Crete, uncostly and reusable until baked. As we will see in Section 6, the majority of inscriptions on clay appear on small rectangular tablets and a variety of sealings, incised with a stylus (or comparable pointed tool).

Both tablets (Section 6.1.1) and sealings (Section 6.1.2) functioned as records of economic transactions for the administration of palatial centres. Lending itself to being reworked at need, clay allowed for flexibility of information recording until the written documents were stored in temporary (likely yearly) deposits (or 'archives').[41] Never intentionally baked, these documents outlasted their intended lifespan due to accidental fires during conflagrations (see Section 2). However, there are also examples of intentionally baked clay inscriptions (fewer in number): these are clay vessels (either carved or painted), mostly used as long-term storage containers (Section 6.1.3).

Clay aside, less common writing media are (Section 6.2) stone vessels (of varying sizes and shapes), metal jewellery (gold, silver, bronze) such as hairpins and rings, seals in soft stone (e.g. serpentine), wall plaster and architectural blocks. It is worth noting that although clay tablets and sealings were produced solely for written recording (and thus to receive writing or stamped seals), some other classes of objects (e.g. stone vessels, large clay storage jars called *pithoi*) were also produced (in the majority) without inscription. Writing was therefore applied to these latter classes of objects to make them distinctive in some way.

5.2.2 Classification System

Linear A inscriptions are classified based on support. In the conventional classification system, each writing medium is assigned an abbreviation (corresponding to its 'class designation') to ease identification of inscriptions' supports at first sight (without requiring access to images). Class designation is preceded by an abbreviation of the inscription's findplace (e.g. HT = Haghia Triada, KH = Khania)[42] and followed by a unique classification number (reference number). The combination of these elements gives us a unique inscription's 'ID-card', used both to retrieve the inscription in edited corpora and reference it in publications.

---

[41] In the Aegean context, 'administrative archives' contain documents needed for day-to-day administration, while 'deposits' are collections of documents found in magazines/workshops (Schoep 2002: 24–6). This nomenclature stems from Linear B scholarship, but does not accurately cover the contexts in which Linear A documents were discovered: 'archive' implies a systematic collection designed for reference, but in most cases Linear A documents were not found in such contexts, nor in the same quantities as their Linear B equivalents.

[42] A list of findplace abbreviations is given in Section 3, Table 2.

Table 3 Writing media classification system[43]

| Designation | | Document type | Example |
Class	Subclass		
–	–	Clay tablets (page-shaped, bars, lames)	HT 100
W– Clay sealings	Wa	Nodules (single-hole hanging nodules) / *noduli*	KH Wa 1001
	Wb	Sealings/flat-based nodules	KN Wb 33
	Wc	Roundels	KH Wc 2001
	Wd	Two-hole hanging nodules	HT Wd 1617
	We	Dome *noduli*	SAM We 4
	Wg	Miscellaneous 'roundels'	PH Wg 45
	Wy	Miscellaneous nodules	PH Wy 42
Z–Vessels and other supports	Za	Stone vessels	IO Za 2
	Zb	Clay vessels with incised inscriptions	KE Zb 4
	Zc	Clay vessels with inked/ painted inscriptions	KN Zc 6
	Zd	Graffiti	HT Zd 155
	Ze	Architecture	KN Ze 45
	Zf	Metal objects with incised inscriptions	KN Zf 13
	Zg	Stone objects	CR Zg 4
	Zh	Ivory objects	KN Zg 57–8[44]

Despite this material variety, it should always be borne in mind that, statistically speaking, Linear A inscriptions are not distributed evenly across all writing media. In other words, not all the writing media listed above bear an equal number of inscriptions. The great majority of inscriptions (96 per cent) occur on five media only: single-hole hanging nodules (ca. just under 900), tablets (ca. 450), roundels (ca. 150), clay vessels (ca. 70) and stone vessels (ca. 50) (Decorte 2018b: 20–2). Last but not the least, in addition to the extant writing media and materials, we may also infer the

---

[43] After Schoep 2002: 13–17; Younger 2024 (*Linear A Texts: Introduction*, section 3, 'Conventions').
[44] Recently published in Kanta et al. 2024.

existence of other writing supports that have not survived to us (but are likely to have existed). In fact, we do have indirect evidence for the use of perishable materials such as parchment and perhaps also papyrus (see Section 9).

5.3 Writing Techniques and Implements

Writing techniques and implements are contingent upon writing media, which thus represent a physical constraint on making inscriptions and influence their visual outcome. Clay can be either 'incised' or 'painted'. Most Linear A clay inscriptions are incised with a stylus (perhaps of metal, ivory, reed or arguably also a thorn); a few are painted with a brush. Neither implement has survived in the archaeological record (there are, however, examples of styluses from the Mycenaean period).[45] Clay can also be 'stamped' with seals (although very few seals are also inscribed; see Section 6.2.5). The other durable writing media bearing Linear A inscriptions (stone, metal, ivory) are 'carved', most likely with chisels or finer cutting tools (e.g. knives, burins, awls, blades), for which there is no uncontroversial archaeological evidence either.[46] The combination of medium, implement and technique (Table 4) brings forth different Linear A 'writing styles', resulting in 'writing traditions' (Schoep 2002: 13): a 'pinacological tradition' (clay inscriptions), an 'epigraphic tradition' (inscriptions on other durable materials), a 'papyrological tradition' (inscriptions on perishable materials). The latter, showing a more cursive style of writing, has barely survived (painted clay inscriptions)[47] but is likely to have existed (see Section 9).

6 (Beyond) Accounting: What Was Linear A Used For?

Studying Linear A necessarily means studying 'inscriptions', but what exactly is an 'inscription'? By convention, an inscription is a sequence of at least two or more signs, forming a word. This definition, however, may be too restrictive as it does not encompass the category of 'single signs' (i.e. signs occurring in isolation; e.g. potmarks, mason's marks, transaction signs, etc.; *GORILA* I: xi clearly excludes these categories). In Aegean scripts, single signs are not unusual, and at times a single sign may function as the abbreviation of a word (e.g. Linear B sign AB 61, with the phonetic value /o/,

---

[45] Images in Palaima 2011: 110–12.

[46] On Minoan crafting tools, see Evely 2000 (esp. figure 76). Rice (in press) explores which tools may have been used to create stone vessels and engrave them with Linear A inscriptions. Very few examples of tools survive in the archaeological record, most of which are argued to have been used to work stone (but are not straightforwardly associated with engraving).

[47] Palaima (1987: 499–500) suggests that Linear A was primarily meant to be written in ink because of its many cursive-looking sign-shapes.

Table 4 Synoptic overview of Linear A writing media, techniques and implements

Writing media			Inscription	
Evidence	**Material**	**Document type**	**Technique**	**Implement**
Direct evidence: Preserved	Clay	Tablets	Incised	Stylus?
		Sealings	Incised, stamped	Stylus?
		Vessels	Incised, painted	Brush, stylus?
	Stone	Vessels	Carved	Carving tools
		Seals	Carved	Carving tools
	Metal	Jewellery	Carved	Carving tools
	Bone	Fragment, disk/ sceptre	Carved	Carving tools
	Plaster	Mural graffiti	Incised	Stylus?
Indirect evidence: Likely existed	Parchment/ leather	Folded sheets	Painted (ink?)	Brush?
Inferable evidence: May have existed	Papyrus	Rolls	Painted (ink?)	Brush?

stands for the word *o-pe-ro* 'deficit'). Therefore, single signs (especially when occurring in isolation, like potmarks) may well deserve to be upgraded to 'inscriptions'. This circumstance has recently made scholars challenge the traditional definition of 'inscription' provided previously in favour of a more comprehensive one including both single-sign and multi-sign texts (Donnelly 2022: 63–5). Most Linear A inscriptions are multi-sign texts. There are, however, instances of single signs occurring in isolation (e.g. potmarks, mason's marks, transaction signs). Given that Linear A is unde-ciphered, it is not always easy to understand whether a single sign abbreviates a word (and therefore has a phonetic meaning) or functions as an ideogram (standing for a concept).

In traditional scholarship, Linear A inscriptions are classified as either 'administrative' or 'non-administrative', thus revealing a (dichotomic) functional approach to taxonomy. For 'administrative' inscriptions, we take all those which come from clearly definable administrative contexts (palatial centres, villas, etc.) and were used to record various kinds of economic transactions. By contrast, all those falling outside this category are taken as 'non-administrative' inscriptions. Needless to say, defining by negation is never a good practice: if the function of an 'administrative' inscription is to record a transaction, then what precisely is the function of a 'non-administrative' inscription? There is no univocal answer – and no short answer either. Before discussing what these inscriptions are, let us first look into how (and why) this distinction came about.

First, a quantitative bias most likely played a role: administrative inscriptions significantly outnumber non-administrative ones, and all come from more or less homogeneous contexts, whereas non-administrative inscriptions show considerable heterogeneity in terms of both writing media and contexts. This circumstance had the effect of arranging into a (perhaps unintentional?) hierarchy Linear A inscriptions, prioritising administrative ones over all others: as a result, the latter were squeezed into a less clear-cut category ('non-administrative'). 'Little', however, does not equal 'belittle': contemporary users of the Linear A script may not have shared our same perception and hierarchy of uses of the objects bearing Linear A writing. Second comes a qualitative bias. The systematisation of Linear A as we know it (script, signary, document types, functions, etc.) is much indebted to Linear B: once Linear B was deciphered (1952) and systematised, the same interpretative (and taxonomic) framework was retrospectively applied to Linear A (see esp. Salgarella 2020: 25–32). Linear B inscriptions are almost exclusively administrative to the point that, compared to Linear A, Linear B is often said to show a restricted context of use (i.e. administrative-only). This, as we have seen, does not necessarily hold true for Linear A and is further proof that an 'administrative' versus 'non-administrative' classification of Linear A evidence is ill-fitting. It has to be borne in mind that in most cases we still see Linear A through the lens of Linear B.

Any classification therefore has to be taken just as a heuristic tool to systematise the extant evidence, and to identify and evaluate patterns. Here the decision has been made to present the rich heterogeneity of Linear A inscriptions based on document type, therefore following a typological classification giving justice to (and accounting for) both the function performed by an inscription and its material aspects (without necessarily implying a functional hierarchy). Inscriptions on clay will be presented first, given that clay is the most common writing support/medium (see Section 5), followed by inscriptions on a variety of other supports.

6.1 Inscriptions on Clay

Inscriptions on clay represent 90 per cent of the extant Linear A corpus, and their function is primarily 'administrative'.

6.1.1 Tablets

Tablets are the most well-known category of 'administrative' documents (a list of findplaces is given in Section 3, Table 2). Tablet deposits (or archives)[48] have been found on Crete at Hagia Triada, Khania, Zakros, Phaistos, Knossos, Malia, Archanes, Tylissos, Palaikastro, Gournia, Papoura, Petras and Pyrgos, on the Aegean islands at Akrotiri (Thera), Hagia Irini (Kea) and Phylakopi (Melos).

Typologically, most Linear A tablets are 'page-shaped' (e.g. HT 118, *GORILA* I: 200–1): small, rectangular documents fitting into the palm of a hand, often inscribed on both sides (hence called 'opisthographs': e.g. ZA 10a–b, *GORILA* III: 168–71).[49] Several tablets are also 'palimpsests' (esp. tablets from Haghia Triada, e.g. HT 115, *GORILA* I: 188–91), meaning that an original inscription was subsequently erased for another one to be superimposed (traces of erased signs are sometimes visible; e.g. HT 115a, lower half, HT 86b, lower half). This suggests that Linear A tablets were often reused (with the older text perhaps copied onto another document for long-term recording, before its being erased to accommodate new information) and thus meant to be temporary records, which survived to us only because of accidental fires (see Section 2). There are also a few examples of 'oblong tablets' and 'bars' (the latter being a document type typical of Cretan Hieroglyphic administration): these only come from Knossos, Phaistos and Mallia (e.g. MA 1a–c, *GORILA* I: 268–9), and all predate the Late Minoan I period (Middle Minoan IIB–IIIB), to which the majority of Linear A evidence is dated (see Section 2).

Tablets were used as records of economic transactions ('recording documents') to keep track of the inflow and outflow of goods within palatial administrations. Their content could be either miscellaneous (multiple commodities) or specialised (single commodity) (for a classification based on

---

[48] On the use of the terms 'archive' and 'deposit' in Linear A, see fn. 41.

[49] For a synoptic overview of Linear A tablets (line-drawings), see *SigLA* (under 'Browse corpus'). On the differences between Linear A and Linear B tablets, see esp. Tomas 2011a.

format types, see Schoep 2002: 67–88; for Haghia Triada tablets, see Montecchi 2019). Among the main basic commodities that we can identify with certainty (through ideograms),[50] there are grains (AB 120/*GRAnum*: grain, probably barley; A 303: grain, probably wheat;[51] AB 65/*FAR*: spelt), olives (AB 122/*OLIVa*), olive oil (A 302/*OLEum*), figs (AB 30/*FICus*), wine (AB 131/*VINum*), vessels (A 400^{VASum}–418^{VASum}), wool (A 556-563/*LANA*), textiles (AB 54/*TELA*, AB 164), animals (livestock: AB 23/*BOS*; sheep: AB 21/*OVIS*; goats: AB 22/*CAPer*; pigs: AB 85/*SUS*), as well as allocations of foodstuff to personnel (AB 100/*VIR*; Schoep 2002: 176–89).

Three main types of transactions can be expected to be represented in the Linear A tablets and are at times positively identified (Schoep 2002: 90–1). These are (i) 'inventories' (and 'assessments') of produce/products (e.g. foodstuff, raw materials, finished products) stored in magazines and workshops located within (or in the vicinity of) the palatial centre, or delivered to the centre from the surrounding areas (e.g. goods produced there and/or information on flocks pastured on them); (ii) 'contribution or collection records' booking the inflow of goods and the contributions made to the central administration (e.g. taxes, levies, deliveries, etc.; although these are not often straightforwardly identifiable); (iii) 'allocation or distribution records' booking the outflow of produce/products (e.g. agricultural commodities, goods, animals, raw materials) from the central administration to different parties (whose purposes may vary: e.g. food rations, payments, etc.; of equally challenging straightforward identification).

Linear A tablets, recording lists of commodities, show a textual structure characterised by an 'opening heading' (usually at tablet-start, but at times headings are placed also elsewhere on a tablet), introducing a section with each entry consisting of one or two words (probably personal or place-names) followed by an ideogram, numbers and fractions. 'Transaction signs/words' (e.g. *KI-RO* 'deficit', *A-DU* 'assessment'; see Section 8.2) and 'simple signs' (of unclear function) can also occur in the text (see Sections 7.1 and 8.2). This basic (theoretical) textual structure may take different (pragmatic) forms based

---

⁵⁰ See the list in the online supplementary appendix, the URL for which is provided in the frontmatter. (where the Latin names of ideograms are also provided)

⁵¹ The correct identification of wheat and barley in Linear B and Linear A is still questioned (on the debate, see esp. Palmer 1992: 482–3; Halstead 1995; Schoep 2002: 104–12; Killen 2004: 160–8; Killen 2024b: 534; Palmer 2008: 625–68; de Fidio 2024). In Linear B, the traditional interpretation (standardly used) is AB 120/*GRAnum* 'wheat' and B 121/*HORDeum* 'barley' (a Linear B-only sign), although convincing arguments have been put forward in support of the opposite reading (i.e. AB 120 'barley' and B 121 'wheat'). To avoid misunderstanding, in this work the generic term 'grain' is used for both AB 120/*GRA* and A 303, until consensus is reached in the academic debate.

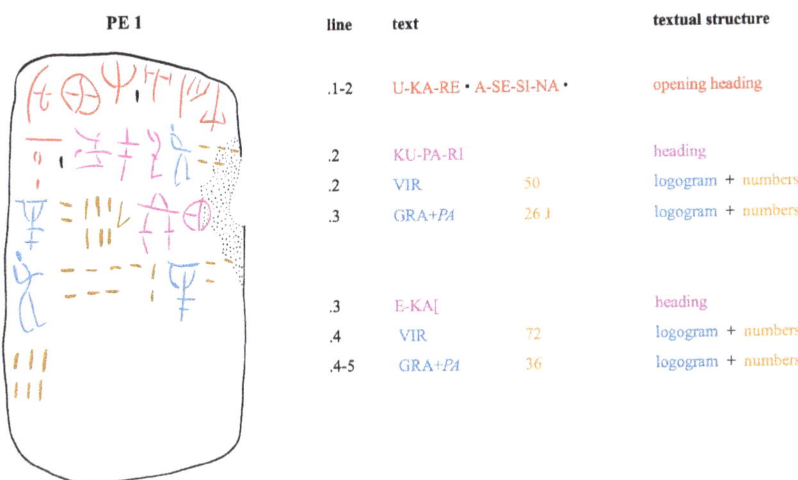

Figure 6 Example of a Linear A tablet's textual structure (PE 1).[52]

on which elements are present on a contextual basis (see the example in Figure 6; see also Section 7.1) and shows considerable cross-site variation. In other words, despite the overall structural similarities, there is no standard textual structure/format that may be applied to all Linear A tablets.

Tablets' textual structure (format types) may give us insights into the process of information recording and related administrative procedures. Some format types may in fact reflect consecutive stages in the information processing system, while other types seem to reflect a specific type of information and are thus likely to have been compiled for different purposes (e.g. recording the purpose of the booking or the administrative status of the commodities; see esp. Schoep 2002: 86–7). It is likely that at the end of the administrative cycle, the information contained on tablets was transferred onto documents of perishable material (see Section 9), functioning as long(er)-term records (to which single-hole hanging nodules may have been attached; see Sections 6.1.2 and 9.1).[53]

6.1.2 Sealings

Sealings are small lumps of clay bearing one or more seal impressions and (at times) writing. They come in a variety of shapes, which can be grouped into four

---

[52] Drawing by Salgarella. Tablet published in Tsipopoulou and Hallager 1996: 25–30 (not in *GORILA*).

[53] For a conjectural reconstruction of the Linear A information processing system, see Schoep 2002: 192–7.

main categories: roundels, *noduli*, flat-based nodules and hanging nodules (further subdivided into single-hole and two-hole; Hallager 1996, I: 21–4, figure 2). The first two categories are 'active' sealings (free-standing documents) playing a role in the transmission of goods, while the latter two categories are 'passive' sealings (auxiliary documents) fastened to goods or written documents (Schoep 2002: 193). Although the precise function(s) of these document types are not yet fully understood, we have a working knowledge of their use (Hallager 1990, 1996, 2010, 2021; Schoep 2002: 192–9; Tomas 2008, 2012; Finlayson 2013, 2018, 2020; Montecchi 2017, 2018).

Roundels (small clay disks; e.g. GO Wc 1, *GORILA* II: 2) and *noduli* (small clay lumps; e.g. HT We/Wc 3020, *GORILA* II: 78; HT We/Wa 1020–1, *GORILA* II: 7) were not meant to be fastened to other items (unlike the other three categories of sealings) and are understood to have worked as independent documents meant to authorise transactions. Roundels functioned as receipts for outgoing or incoming goods[54] (reflecting the 'internal' movement of goods within each palatial system): it has been argued that the number of seal impressions on a roundel's rim may specify the quantity of the commodity recorded in the inscription occurring on one or both of its sides, with each impression representing one unit (Hallager 1996: 100–1, 113). The seal user would be the recipient of the goods, certifying with the seal impression the units taken (Hallager 1996: 116). Since *noduli* carry one single seal impression, their purpose seems to have been to authenticate one transaction or certify an activity. It has been suggested that *noduli* worked as receipts for work done or tokens to be exchanged for goods or services (Weingarten 1986: 18; 1990: 19–20).

Flat-based nodules (examples in Section 9) show a seal impression (and rarely an inscription) on the upper side and imprints of thread and fibre on underside, suggesting they were pressed against tightly folded parchment (or papyrus?), arguably in order to secure the integrity of the document and prevent unauthorised viewing. Hanging nodules (e.g. HT Wa 1242; *GORILA* II: 25) are understood to have been fastened to a string (moulded around its end if showing a single hole, along its length if showing two holes) tied to goods to be delivered to (or collected from) the palatial centre (thus reflecting the 'external' movement of goods, between the central administration and external parties). Hanging nodules show one (or two) seal impressions on their sides and one/two Linear A sign/s on another side. They most likely served as labels or tags, supplying details about the delivery's content and/or parties

---

[54] See Weingarten 2017 for the argument that roundels reflect incoming products or materials.

involved, or production/destination places (Krzyszkowska 2005: 160; Montecchi 2017; Hallager 1996: 197–9 for the suggestion that one-hole hanging nodules sealed papyrus documents; see also Section 9.1). Finally, in addition to these main categories, we also have 'direct object sealings' (e.g. HT Wb 2001, *GORILA* II: 70; PH Wb 36, *GORILA* II: 92): these are lumps of clay attached to objects (jars, wooden or wicker baskets, or over pegs securing chests or doors) and impressed with a seal to secure their content or integrity (the seal impression would identify the individual responsible for the action' Krzyszkowska 2005: 28).

Regarding the Linear A information processing system, there is no compelling nor probative evidence to suggest that the information held on sealed documents was later transferred onto tablets (which instead happens in the Linear B administrative practice). Thus Linear A sealed documents and tablets are unlikely to reflect consecutive stages of information processing. Rather, they are likely to have acted as complementary, parallel sets of documents within the administrative system and, arguably, to reflect different administrative concerns: tablets appear to relate to obligations concerning agricultural commodities, whereas sealed documents relate to different kinds of transactions involving a different (perhaps wider) geographical scale, or matters of different administrative status (Schoep 2002: 197).

6.1.3 Clay Vessels

Inscriptions on clay vessels can be either incised (e.g. TY Zb 4, *GORILA* IV: 109) or, more rarely, painted (e.g. Knossos 'conical cups': KN Zc 6–7, *GORILA* IV: 118–25; images in Flouda 2013: 160; 2015: 78; Dimopoulou-Rethemiotaki 2005: 217). It is worth noting that the majority of incised inscriptions on clay vessels were made before firing, meaning that they were part of the vessel's manufacture. Although most clay vessels were found in cultic contexts and are therefore likely to have fulfilled cultic/ritual purposes, there are a number of inscriptions on large storage jars (*pithoi*) that clearly indicate their content (e.g. showing the ideogram for 'wine').

6.1.4 Clay Figurines

Deposited in cultic contexts (mostly peak sanctuaries or temple repositories), figurines most likely performed a dedicatory function (see esp. Morris 2017; Peatfield and Morris 2020), but only very few bear inscriptions (e.g. TY Zg 1, *GORILA* IV: 170; Flouda 2015: 70). Interestingly, the latest attestation of Linear A (ca. 1350 BCE) is a painted (cursive-looking) inscription (retrograde) on a figurine from Poros Herakleios (PO Zc 1; Dimopoulou et al. 1993).

6.1.5 Functional Objects

Loom weights (made of clay) occasionally bear inscriptions (e.g. from Kythera: KY Zg 1, *GORILA* IV: 166).

6.2 Inscriptions on Other Supports

Inscriptions on other supports represent 10 per cent of the extant Linear A corpus, and their function is mostly 'non-administrative' (most likely cultic, ritual, dedicatory).

6.2.1 Stone Vessels

Stone vessels come in a variety of shapes: circular vessels (SY Za 3, *GORILA* V: 66–7; PK Za 15, *GORILA* IV: 41), stepped vessels (KN Za 10, *GORILA* IV: 8), cylindrical jars (AP Za 2, *GORILA* IV: 4–5), cups (IO Za 6, *GORILA* V: 24–7), libation ladles (TL Za 1, *GORILA* IV: 58–9) and libation tables of various sizes (IO Za 2, *GORILA* V: 18–9; AP Za 1, *GORILA* IV: 2–3; PK Za 11, *GORILA* IV: 32–4). Of these, only around fifty are inscribed (Davis 2014: 17–66; Decorte 2018b: 20–1), and are mostly libation tables and ladles showing the so-called 'libation formula' (see Sections 7 and 8). Libation tables and ladles were used for pouring liquid offerings during cultic activities and performative rites, and often bear votive inscriptions suggesting a ceremonial use of Linear A (for their uses, see Davis 2014: 99–142). Inscribed tables represent a considerable minority of the total, suggesting they were offered by a restricted group of individuals (Flouda 2013: 164). Most inscribed stone vessels come from cultic contexts, thus suggesting they performed a ritual purpose: extra-urban 'peak' sanctuaries (Petsofas, Iouktas, Vrysinas and Haghios Georgios on Kythera), the Psychro cave, the Kato Syme shrine (Davis 2014: 17–59). Fewer inscribed stone vessels have been found in urban contexts: at Knossos, Apodoulou, Roussolakkos, Palaikastro, Prasa, Troullos and Nerokourou (Davis 2014: 59–67; Karnava 2016: 348).

6.2.2 Metal Objects

A few metal objects, all coming from non-administrative contexts (cemeteries, caves), bear inscriptions: a bronze bowl (KO Zf 2, *GORILA* IV: 158–9), silver and gold 'double axes' (e.g. AR Zf 1–2, *GORILA* IV: 142–3), silver and gold pins (e.g. PL Zf 1, *GORILA* IV: 161–2; KN Zf 31, *GORILA* IV: 154–5; CR Zf 1, *GORILA* IV: 146–7; ARKH Zf 9, Sakellaraki et al. 2018), a gold ring (KN Zf 13, *GORILA* IV: 152–3; images in Flouda 2013: 161–2; 2015: 7; Dimopoulou-Rethemiotaki 2005: 219). These objects are likely to have played a role in elite conspicuous consumption. Extant are also inscribed copper/bronze ingots from Haghia Triada (e.g. HT Zf 163–8; images in Dimopoulou-Rethemiotaki 2005: 211) and a metal weight (ca. 1,450 kg) from Mochlos (MO Zf 1; Schoep 2002: 35).

6.2.3 Graffiti

At Hagia Triada, fragments of a fallen wall plaster show traces of writing (HT Zd 155–7, *GORILA* IV: 130–5; Duhoux 1998: 8), suggesting more widespread uses of Linear A (outside a strict 'administrative' versus 'non-administrative' context).

6.2.4 Architectural Elements

A few stone blocks show Linear A signs: a square block from Kophinas (KO Za 1, *GORILA* IV: 18–20) and blocks later incorporated in a wall at Mallia (Pelon 1980: 224, no. 301). A block of the Kephala tomb (KN Ze 16, *GORILA* IV: 138) bears signs equally readable as either Linear A or Linear B.

6.2.5 Soft Stone and Ivory

Unlike Cretan Hieroglyphic, Linear A is rarely engraved on sealstones, of which only a few examples are known (ARM Zg 1, *CMS* V Suppl. IB, no. 310; KN Zg 55, *CMS* II.2, no. 213b; CR(?) Zg 3, *CMS* XI, no. 311; CR Zg 4, *CMS* XII, no. 96; see Del Freo 2005: 663–5; Decorte 2018b: 26, fn. 37). From Haghios Stephanos (mainland Greece) comes an inscribed schist fragment (HS Zg 1, *GORILA* V: 16). There is also some evidence for ivory as writing support: a small bar (or 'tag') from Zakros (ZA Zg 35, published in Kopaka 1989) and the recently discovered 'Knossos Disk' (KN Zg 57–8, published in Kanta et al. 2024) made of hippopotamus tusk. This find is argued to be part of a 'sceptre' used for ritual/cultic purposes.

7 'Elementary, My Dear Watson': What Do We Know from Reading Linear A?

Although Linear A has not yet been deciphered, we can still make sense of the texts (to an extent and with approximation) thanks to several cumulative factors, by (i) analysing Linear A itself and (ii) comparing it with Linear B.

The contexts of use of Linear A documents ('administrative' or 'cultic' texts; see Sections 5 and 6) allow us to 'predict' (to an extent) which kind of information to expect. Internal analysis of Linear A textual structure (see Section 8) can help identify recurrent structures (and words), whose probable meaning may then be deduced based on context (given the short, formulaic nature of Linear A texts). Iconographic analysis (underpinned by comparison with real-world referents, coming from either the archaeological record or the natural environment) can help identify the commodities represented by ideograms.

Linear B offers insightful *comparanda* in terms of administrative and economic systems (largely continued from the earlier period of 'Minoan' administration). Linear A/B shared ideograms (see Schoep 2002: 94–135; Salgarella 2020: 219–20, 225–6) give us a general understanding of the Linear A commodities recorded on tablets. Linear A/B shared personal names and place-names, along with terms understood to belong in the Minoan substratum, add up to our short 'Pocket Minoan Dictionary' (see Section 8).

For these reasons, we are currently in a position to 'read' Linear A texts to an extent and with some degree of confidence, despite not knowing the grammatical structures, as well as linguistic affiliation, of the Minoan language (see Section 8). Given that Linear A is 'readable' and the contents of its texts are understandable to the extent possible given the present evidence, we propose here a '*reading*[+] approach' to Linear A documents, allowing for a reading and tentative, plausible interpretation of the Linear A texts, without however supplying a literal 'translation' thereof.

7.1 *Reading*[+] a Linear A tablet

As illustrative examples of Linear A tablets, we will look at three tablets from Haghia Triada, a site which has yielded the best-preserved evidence allowing for (relatively) substantial reading and interpretation of the preserved texts. These are HT 28 (Section 7.1.1), HT 120 (Section 7.1.2) and HT 121 (Section 7.1.3).

7.1.1 HT 28

One of the best-preserved documents, HT 28a–b (Figures 7–8), is a page-shaped tablet from Haghia Triada, dated to Late Minoan IB. It records mixed agricultural commodities and is inscribed on both sides with very similar texts. Hence, it is understood to be a 'balance ledger' tablet – that is, a transaction document recording contributions made to the centre (side a) and debts/deficits/future payments (side b). The original assessment (i.e. how much produce the centre had originally requested) can therefore be reconstructed by totalling contributions (side a) and outstanding debts (side b).

Although the language behind Linear A is not deciphered, we can still make sense (approximately) of the contents of the tablet, thanks to its textual structure (layout), comparative analysis with other administrative records and the ideograms it shows (giving us an overview of the commodities recorded; see also Section 6.1.1). To begin with, the same agricultural commodities are listed on both sides (ideograms,

---

Tablet information

Type:　　　　　Page-shaped tablet (5.9 cm × 8.5 cm × 0.9 cm; drawings not to scale)
Findplace:　　Haghia Triada, Villa (Room 72)
Period:　　　　Late Minoan IB
Classification: Mixed Commodities Tablet
　　　　　　　　(Schoep 2002: 81, Type IA; Montecchi 2010: 34, Class Mb)
Edited in:　　*GORILA* I: 52–3

Side a (front)　　　　　　　　　　　　　**Side b (back)**

(a)

(b)

Figure 7 HT 28a–b.[55]

plain or ligatured with syllabograms) in almost a fixed order (which is a typical feature of Haghia Triada's 'mixed commodities tablets'; see also Section 7.1.3): grain (AB 120/*GRA*), olive oil (A 302/*OLE*), figs (AB 30/*FIC*), wine (AB 131a/*VIN*) and an unidentified commodity (A 304; Figure 8). We can 'read' and 'interpret' these ideograms as they were continued in Linear B (except for A 304).

Then, three words (in red, Figure 8) may be taken as transaction terms (see Sections 4 and 8): *A-SI-JA-KA* and *SA-RA₂* (occurring on both sides) and *U-MI-NA-SI* (on side b). *A-SI-JA-KA* starts the text on both sides: although (most unluckily) this term is a one-off attestation in the known Linear A vocabulary, it may be argued to be a transaction term because of its marked position and repetition at text-start on both sides. *A-SI-JA-KA* is therefore likely to function as a 'heading' (see Section 6.1.1), referring to the whole record. *SA-RA₂* (occurring on both sides: side a, line .3; side b, line .2) is likely to be a transaction term as it functions (mostly) as such on comparative evidence (Schoep 2002: 164–6). *U-MI-NA-SI* (on side b, split across lines .1 and .2) arguably belongs in this category, given its position after *A-SI-JA-KA* and between dots (where transaction signs usually occur). In fact, the

---

[55] Drawings by Salgarella.

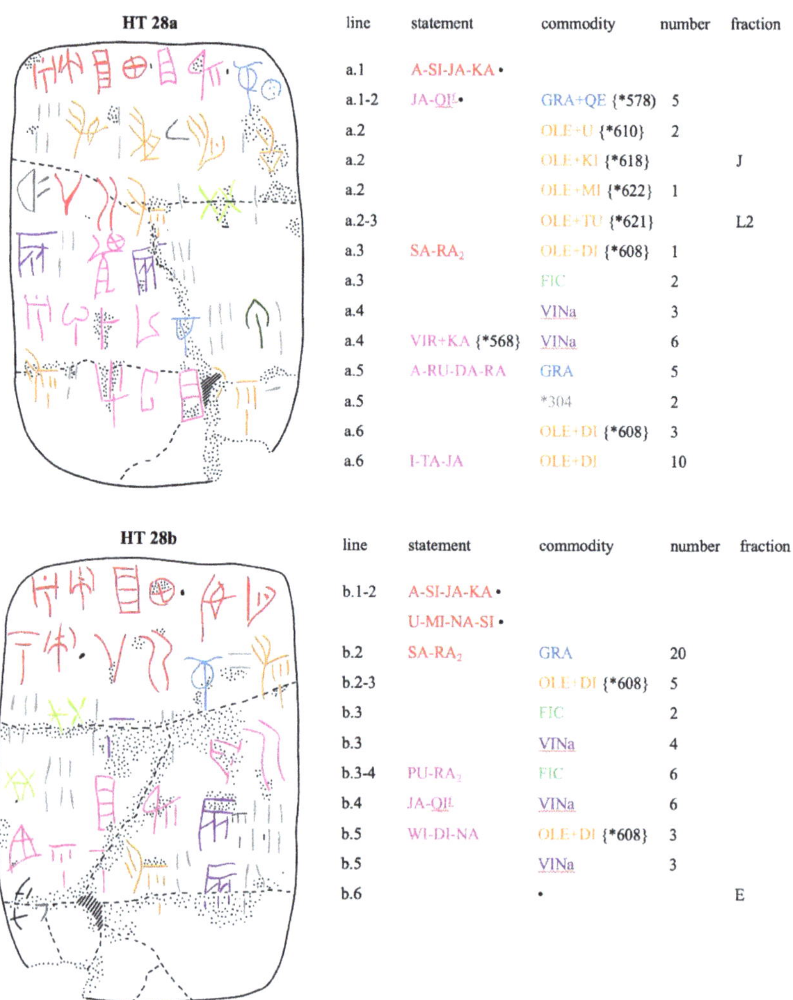

HT 28a

line	statement	commodity	number	fraction
a.1	A-SI-JA-KA •			
a.1-2	JA-QIᵉ •	GRA+QE {*578}	5	
a.2		OLE+U {*610}	2	
a.2		OLE+KI {*618}		J
a.2		OLE+MI {*622}	1	
a.2-3		OLE+TU {*621}		L2
a.3	SA-RA₂	OLE+DI {*608}	1	
a.3		FIC	2	
a.4		VINa	3	
a.4	VIR+KA {*568}	VINa	6	
a.5	A-RU-DA-RA	GRA	5	
a.5		*304	2	
a.6		OLE+DI {*608}	3	
a.6	I-TA-JA	OLE+DI	10	

HT 28b

line	statement	commodity	number	fraction
b.1-2	A-SI-JA-KA •			
	U-MI-NA-SI •			
b.2	SA-RA₂	GRA	20	
b.2-3		OLE+DI {*608}	5	
b.3		FIC	2	
b.3		VINa	4	
b.3-4	PU-RA₂	FIC	6	
b.4	JA-QIᵉ	VINa	6	
b.5	WI-DI-NA	OLE+DI {*608}	3	
b.5		VINa	3	
b.6	•			E

Figure 8 Textual structure of HT 28a–b.[56]

mixed-commodities textual format is usually characterised (at least on Haghia Triada tablets) by a heading often followed by a transaction sign (or term) and a list of individual entries (sign-sequence + ideogram + numbers). *U-MI-NA-SI* has been suggested to mean 'debt' or '[s/he] owes'.[57] But who are the parties involved, giving contributions and owing debts? Most arguably, these are hidden behind the remaining words (in pink, Figure 8): *JA-QI* (on both sides: side a, line .1; side b, line .4); *VIR+KA*, *A-RU-DA-RA* and *I-TA-JA* (side a, lines .4 to .6); *PU-RA₂* and

---

[56] Drawings by Salgarella; phonetic transcription adapted from Younger 2024 (*Linear A Texts in Phonetic Transcription: Haghia Triada*).

[57] Younger 2024 (*Linear A Texts: Introduction*, section 9b, 'Transaction Words').

WI-DI-NA (side b, lines .3, .5). It has been suggested that these words may be women's names: they all end in -*A*, arguably a feminine ending (Godart 1984: 125; Schoep 2002: 113, fn. 81; Younger 2024, *Linear A Texts in Phonetic Transcription: Haghia Triada*, under section HT 28). Finally, can we reconstruct the original assessment? If we assume that side a records actual disbursements while side b records deficits, by totalling their respective figures we would have thirty units (+ *J E L₂* sub-units) of grain, twenty-five units of oil, ten units of figs, sixteen units of wine and six units of wine associated with *VIR+KA* (perhaps 'porters'?; Godart 1984: 125).

7.1.2 HT 120

Tablet HT 120 (Figure 9) was unearthed at the site of Haghia Triada and is dated to Late Minoan IB. HT 120 is classified as a 'specialised commodity tablet' (Schoep 2002: 82), meaning that it specialises in recording a single commodity (and/or its variants).

Tablet information

Type:　　　　　　Page-shaped tablet (5.3 cm × 8.3 cm × 0.9 cm; drawing not to scale)
Findplace:　　　 Haghia Triada, Casa del Lebete
Period:　　　　　Late Minoan IB
Classification: Specialised Commodities Tablet
　　　　　　　　　(Schoep 2002: 82, Type II; Montecchi 2010: 33, Class Eb)
Edited in:　　　 *GORILA* I: 204–5

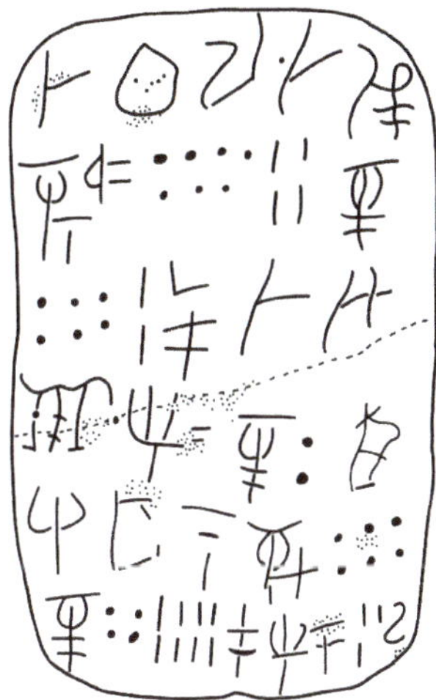

Figure 9 HT 120.[58]

---

[58] Drawing by Salgarella.

Tablets belonging in the 'specialised commodity' format type mostly focus on agricultural commodities, namely olive oil (A 302/*OLE*), olives (AB 122/*OLIV*), a grain (AB 120/*GRA*)[59] and A 308 (non-identified commodity). Their textual structure is characterised by consecutive entries consisting of sign-sequences (i.e. words) followed by ideograms, numerals and fractional signs (at times words are omitted and only ideograms and numerals/fractions appear). HT 120 specialises in recording a grain (AB 120/*GRA*) and variants thereof (in the form of complex/composite signs constructed around AB 120). The textual structure of HT 120 is given in Figure 10.

The textual structure of HT 120 shows the pattern 'word + ideogram + numbers/fractions' in all entries, which are arguably preceded by an 'opening heading' (see Section 6.1.1), namely *DA-QE-RA* (in bright red in Figure 10, line .1), the meaning of which is unclear (but perhaps a transaction term). The opening heading is graphically delimited by a punctuation mark (in the shape of a dot). The following entries are all introduced by a word (in pink in Figure 10): *DA-ME* (line .1), *DA-U-*49* (split across lines .3-.4), *KI-RE-TA-NA* (split across lines .4-.5) and *PA-I-TO* (line .6). Of these, only *PA-I-TO* can be interpreted with some degree of

HT 120	line	statement	commodity	number	fraction
	.1	DA-QE-RA •			
	.1-2	DA-ME	GRA+K+L$_2$ {*584}	74	
	.2-3		GRA+PA {*574}	62	J A
	.3-4	DA-U-*49 • I	GRA+PA {*574}	20	
	.4-5	KI-RE-TA-NA	GRA+B {*580}	60	
	.6		GRA+PA {*574}	48	
	.6	PA-I-TO		3	D

Figure 10 Textual structure of HT 120.[60]

---

⁵⁹ See fn. 51.

⁶⁰ Drawing by Salgarella; phonetic transcription adapted from Younger 2024 (*Linear A Texts in Phonetic Transcription: Haghia Triada*).

certainty: this is most likely a place-name, referring to the site of Phaistos in central Crete.[61] By inference, we may suppose that the other words are also place-names. In particular, *DA-U-*49* is argued to correspond to the place-name *da-wo*, often found in the Linear B tablets in association with Phaistos.[62]

Each one of these words (perhaps all place-names) is followed by one or more (complex/composite) ideograms featuring AB 120/*GRA* (grain):[63] A 584 (line .2) and A 580 (line 5.) consists of AB 120/*GRA* followed by one or more fractional signs (conventionally transcribed as *K*, L_2, *B*; see the list of fractional signs in the online supplementary appendix, the URL for which is provided in the frontmatter), whereas A 574 (lines .2, .4, .6) ligatures A 120/*GRA* with AB 03/*PA* (whose two horizontal lines can be recognised in the stalk of AB 120/*GRA*). It has been suggested (Schoep 2002: 154) that AB 120/*GRA* may have functioned as a land measure (as it does in Linear B) when modified by fractions (in our case, A 584 and A 580), whereas ligatures of AB 120/*GRA* with a syllabic sign (e.g. A 574) may refer to specific aspects of the grain (e.g. 'milled', 'raw', 'processed', 'fodder', etc.). Ligature *GRA+PA* (= A 574) is always recorded in small quantities, and elsewhere (PE 1, given in Figure 6, Section 6.1.1) this produce is arguably allocated to personnel (AB 100/*VIR*) in half units (Schoep 2002: 106, 108). Hence, *GRA+PA* may perhaps stand for 'processed' grain (food ration for human consumption). Finally, the text of HT 120 shows a simple (or transaction) sign: this is AB 28/*I* (line .4; in dark red in Figure 10), preceded by a punctuation mark (in the shape of a dot). The meaning of AB 28/*I* in this context is unclear: if it works as a transaction sign, it may be an indication of the type of transaction (e.g. assessment, contribution, disbursement, etc.) being recorded.

7.1.3 HT 121

Tablet HT 121 (Figure 11) was unearthed at the site of Haghia Triada and is dated to Late Minoan IB.

Like HT 28 (see Section 7.1.1), HT 121 is classified as a 'mixed commodities tablet' (Schoep 2002: 81), a format type characterised by a wide

---

[61] It has also been suggested (Bennet 1992: 92, fn. 97; Petrakis 2014: 59–60) that in Late Minoan III the place-name *pa-i-to* refers to the nearby site of Haghia Triada (not Phaistos) as more active and thriving.

[62] Younger 2024 (*Linear A Texts: Introduction*, section 10c, 'Place Names'). On Linear A *DA-U-*49* and Linear B *da-wo*, see Palaima 1994. On the interpretation and possible location of Linear B place-name *da-wo*, see esp. Monti 2015 and 2019 (*da-wo* = Haghia Triada); Bendall 2017 (*da-wo* = Kommos).

[63] See fn. 51.

Tablet information

Type: Page-shaped tablet (4.1 cm × 6 cm × 1 cm; drawing not to scale)
Findplace: Haghia Triada, Casa del Lebete
Period: Late Minoan IB
Classification: Mixed Commodities Tablet
                 (Schoep 2002: 81, Type IA; Montecchi 2010:34, Class Mc)
Edited in: *GORILA* I: 204–5

Figure 11 HT 121.[64]

range of agricultural commodities booked in a (more or less) fixed order. Usually the order is AB 120/*GRA* and A 303 'grains',[65] A 302/*OLE* 'olive oil', AB 122/*OLIV* 'olives', AB 30/*FIC* 'figs' and AB 131a/*VIN* 'wine' (see also Section 6.1.1). Ideograms aside, the lexical information contained in these tablets is usually minimal (with HT 28a–b being an exception in this respect), as it is mostly limited to a heading, possibly followed by a transaction sign or a transaction term. The textual structure of HT 121 is given in Figure 12.

The text shows two transaction terms (*KI-RI-TA₂* on line .1 and *SA-RA₂* on line .2; in red in Figure 12), each one followed by one or more entries of the type 'ideogram + numbers'. These terms are therefore likely to function as 'headings'. The word *KI-RI-TA₂* is argued to be related to the transaction term *KI-RO* 'deficit' (see also Section 8.2) and to be a verbal form, perhaps meaning

---

[64] Drawing by Salgarella.   [65] See fn. 51.

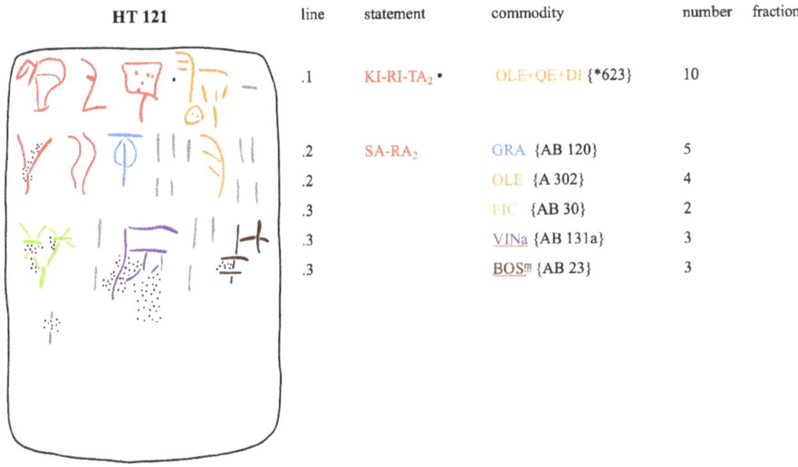

HT 121	line	statement	commodity	number	fraction
	.1	KI-RI-TA₂ •	OLE+QE+DI {*623}	10	
	.2	SA-RA₂	GRA {AB 120}	5	
	.2		OLE {A 302}	4	
	.3		FIC {AB 30}	2	
	.3		VINa {AB 131a}	3	
	.3		BOSᵐ {AB 23}	3	

Figure 12 Textual structure of HT 121.[66]

something like 'is/are lacking'.[67] As noted previously (Section 7.1.1), *SA-RA₂* is likely to be a transaction term whose precise meaning is unclear, as it functions (mostly) as such on comparative evidence (Schoep 2002: 164–6). Most ideograms on HT 121 are plain: on line .2, AB 120/*GRA* 'grain' and A 302/*OLE* 'olive oil', and on line .3, AB 30/*FIC* 'figs', AB 131a/*VIN* 'wine' and AB 23ᵐ/*BOSᵐ* 'oxen' (male 'gendered' variant of AB 23/*BOS*; see Section 4). These are all booked under *SA-RA₂*. The only complex/composite ideogram is A 623 (line .1), a ligature of AB 120/*GRA* 'grain' with syllabic signs AB 78/*QE* and AB 07/*DI*. The meaning of this composite sign is unknown, and note that this is the only commodity booked after *KI-RI-TA₂*. It has been argued that HT 121 (showing a text similar to HT 114) may be related to feasting activities, recording contributions for a communal feast[68] (note that Linear B tablets often record commodities for 'feasting/banqueting'). All commodities are, in fact, booked in whole units. On the assumption that 'Minoan' (Linear A) dry and liquid units are likely to equal 'Mycenaean' (Linear B) dry and liquid units,[69] it can be calculated that the three units of wine booked on HT 121 (line .3) correspond to ca. 86.4 litres (1 liquid unit = ca. 28.8 litres). In turn, if we assume a consumption of ca. 0.25 litres per person (corresponding to two average Minoan 'conical cups'), three units of wine would provide for almost 350 people.[70]

---

[66] Drawing by Salgarella; phonetic transcription adapted from Younger 2024 (*Linear A Texts in Phonetic Transcription: Haghia Triada*).

[67] Younger 2024 (*Linear A Texts: Introduction*). Linear B *ki-ri-ta* is unlikely to be related to the Linear A term (*DMic* s.v.).

[68] Younger 2024 (*Linear A Texts in Phonetic Transcription: Haghia Triada*, section HT 121).

[69] Younger 2003.

[70] Younger 2024 (*Linear A Texts in Phonetic Transcription: Haghia Triada*, section HT 121).

7.2 *Reading*[+] the 'Libation Formula'

The so-called libation formula is the longest Linear A text that has survived, which gives us some valuable insights into the morphology and syntax of the Minoan language (see Section 8). This text is only attested on stone ('libation') vessels, used in cultic (ritual, dedicatory) contexts and activities, and is called 'formula' because of its repetitive structure. The libation formula is therefore standardly classified as a non-administrative text (see Section 6), and is understood to contain a dedicatory sentence or prayer (Davis 2013; Karnava 2016; Younger 2024, *Linear A Texts: Introduction*, under section 12, 'Libation Formula'). An illustrative example of an inscribed libation stone vessel is a 'libation table' (Figure 13), showing cup-shaped hollows into which liquid offerings were poured, and the 'libation formula' running along its edges.

The libation formula comes in two main versions, called 'principal' and 'secondary' (Karetsou, Godart and Olivier 1985: 134), showing a number of sign-sequences (words) in strict order (relative to one another). The principal version is the most common form, standardly showing six sign-sequences, whereas the secondary version is a shortened version consisting of three sign-sequences only. The two versions share one sign-sequence only, reading *A/JA-SA-SA-RA-ME* (with *A-* alternating with *JA-* at word-start on a contextual basis), which has a long history of use. It is attested as *A-SA-SA-RA-NE* in the Arkhanes Script

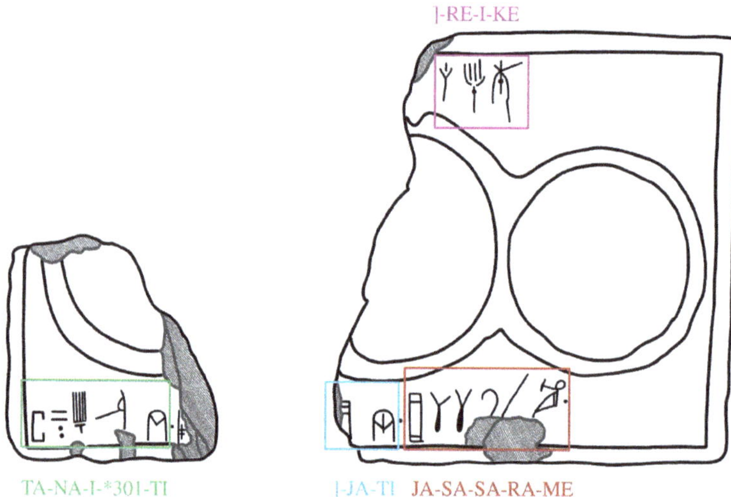

Figure 13 Libation table from the Psykhro Cave showing the libation formula (PS Za 2, *GORILA* IV: 52–5).[71]

---

[71] Drawing by Salgarella.

Table 5 Interpretation of sign-sequences of the libation formula[72]

First	Second	Third	Fourth	Fifth	Sixth
Verb (main)	Place name	Dedicant's name	Object	Verb (subordinate)	Prepositional phrase

(ca. 2000–1800 BCE) and Cretan Hieroglyphic (ca. 1900–1600 BCE), as *A/JA-SA-SA-RA-ME* in Linear A (list of shared attestations given in Civitillo 2016: 165–6) and arguably also in the latest survival of Linear A writing (Poros figurine, ca. 1400 BCE; Dimopoulou et al. 1993; see Section 6.1.4). This shared word is argued to be evidence of continuity in the cultural history of Crete throughout the second millennium BCE (Karnava 2016: 354). The other sign-sequences, instead, show contextual variation. After a comparative study of the sequences' order, Davis (2013) puts forward compelling arguments as to how to interpret the formula's syntax (see also the earlier study by Duhoux 1992), thus suggesting the following readings for each sequence occurring in a fixed position (Table 5).

The longest version ('principal') of the formula shows two clauses starting with a verb (in the first and fifth positions). The first sequence is understood to be the main verb, constructed around a central root (*I-*301*) variably affixed (e.g. *A-TA-I-301, A-TA-I-301-WA-JA, A-TA-I-301-WA-E, TA-NA-I-301-TI, TA-NA-I-301-U-TI-NU*), arguably meaning '(s/he) gives/dedicates'. The second sequence is identified as a place-name (e.g. *DI-KI-TE* 'Mount Dikte', *I-DA* 'Mount Ida', *TU-RI-SA* 'Tylissos'; see also Section 8.2), most likely the location where the dedication was offered. The third sequence is likely to be the dedicant's name (subject of the main clause), as it always changes. The fourth sequence is *A/JA-SA-SA-RA-ME*, taken as the direct object of the sentence, probably meaning 'dedication/offering'. The fifth sequence is argued to be a verb starting a subordinate (dependent) clause and giving a reason for the dedication, thus meaning something like 'hoping for/requesting'. The sixth element is likely to be a prepositional phrase as it shows the suffix *-TE* 'from' (see Section 8.2). Hence a tentative interpretation of the standard version of the formula may be 'gives/dedicates, at [place], [dedicant's name], a dedication/offering, hoping for/requesting, [a favour?] from [a deity?]'.[73] Not all texts of the libation formula show all the elements listed in Table 5 (which is therefore to be taken as a theoretical model), and a few texts show a couple of extra sign-sequences (eight in total). A good example of a well-preserved standard version of the formula is attested on IO Za 2, a libation table from Iouktas (*GORILA* V: 18–19), whose text and interpretation are given in Table 6.

---

[72] After Davis 2013; Younger 2024 (*Linear A Texts: Introduction*, section 12, 'Libation Formula').
[73] Younger 2024 (*Linear A Texts: Introduction*, section 12, 'Libation Formula').

Table 6 Libation formula on IO Za 2[74]

Verb	Subject	Object	Subordinate clause	
*a-ta-i-*301-wa-ja*	*ja-di-ki-tu*	*ja-sa-sa-ra-me*	*u-na-ka-na-si*	*i-pi-na-ma si-ru-te*
'gives'	(dedicant)	'(an) offering'	'requesting'	'(a) favour' 'from (a deity)'

The first three sequences (main verb, dedicant's name and direct object) tend always to be present in all versions of the formula. For instance, in Figure 13 (PS Za 2), showing a shorter version of the formula, we can recognise the verb (*TA-NAI -I-*301-TI*), the dedicant's name (*J-JA-TI*) and the object 'an offering' (*JA-SA-SA-RA-ME*). Given that the formula displays a Verb-Subject-Object (VSO) word-order, Davis (2013: 49) argues that there is a substantial chance for Minoan to be a Verb-Subject-Object (VSO) language (see Section 8).

8 Speaking in Riddles: Which Language Does Linear A Encode?

Although Linear B was successfully deciphered as Greek in 1952, its ancestor Linear A still defies us: which language does Linear A encode? Still hard to say. Scholars have long set out to crack the Linear A code by using a number of different approaches, no one of which has so far given uncontroversial results. Why does Linear A still resist decipherment? There are (unfortunately, we daresay) a number of objective obstacles to deciphering Linear A.

First comes the issue of *quantity*: the extant evidence is scanty (ca. 2,500 inscriptions; see Section 3, Table 2) and in a poor state of preservation (most inscriptions are fragmentary). By contrast, Linear B is much better placed, with more than 4,500 inscriptions, longer and overall better preserved. Second comes the issue of *quality*: Linear A texts are for the most part short and formulaic, showing very little syntax. As illustrated in Section 6, most Linear A 'administrative' documents are terse, brief records of economic transactions (looking like shopping lists); 'non-administrative' inscriptions (for cultic, dedicatory, ritual purposes) show slightly longer texts, which are, however, highly formulaic and repetitive. Although these latter texts are the longest we have and play a significant role in our appreciation of the Minoan language, they are neither extensive nor varied enough for a thorough linguistic investigation of the underlying, constitutive features of the Minoan language. Moreover, there

---

[74] Reading and interpretation by Davis 2013: 46.

appears to be no evidence of Linear A, in our surviving texts, outside of administrative and cultic/ritual contexts: there is no historiography, literature, diplomatic correspondence, monumental inscriptions or private letters written in Linear A (see Section 9). Last but not the least, no bilingual text has so far been found, neither within nor outside of Crete: this means that, on present evidence, there does not exist (perhaps yet?) a 'Rosetta Stone' for Linear A. Hence, overall there is not enough cumulative, probative evidence, in terms of both *quantity* and *quality*, for a successful, convincing and uncontroversial decipherment of Linear A.

In light of these factors, we may ask ourselves: what does it mean 'to decipher' a script? Which conditions are necessary successfully to crack a code? Short answer, 'to decipher' a script means to make sense of its written texts. Well, we can 'make sense' of Linear A text, to an extent and with an approximation (as seen in Section 7); yet, the language Linear A encodes still remains 'undeciphered'. Script decipherment is, in fact, a subtler process. Thus, the longer answer is that deciphering a script requires an accurate understanding of the grammatical structures of the language the script encodes – for example, phonological (phonemes), morphological (word formation), syntactical (sentence formation) structures and systems. It also requires an understanding of the language's position in relation to the already existing linguistic families (i.e. groups of languages of common descent, which share a number of comparable linguistic features).

What has been done in relation to Linear A and the Minoan language? Various methods have been explored to investigate the Minoan language, no one of which (especially if used exclusively) has proven entirely satisfactory nor has it given conclusive and uncontroversial results. The etymological method was the first to be adopted (e.g. Palmer 1958, 1968; Gordon 1966, 1969; Best 1972, 2001; Finkelberg 1990–1; Brown 1990, 1993). This method consists in a lexical comparison between words written in Linear A and the lexicon of known languages used in other (primarily neighbouring) regions (e.g. Semitic, Indo-European, etc.), on the assumption that, should enough similarities be drawn with one of the target languages, this would prove the linguistic affiliation of the Minoan language (written in Linear A) with said target language (and its linguistic family). When applied to Aegean scripts, however, this approach is fraught with problems.

Given that the etymological method consists in comparing Linear A texts (and vocabulary) against known languages, first comes the issue of how to 'restore' (or 'reconstruct') the readings of Linear A sign-sequences (i.e. words) for as accurate a comparison as possible with the lexicon of known target languages. The orthographic conventions of the Linear A syllabary are not yet fully understood, although scholars often work on the assumption that Linear B orthography can also be retrospectively applied (with an approximation) to Linear A: this is, however, not to be taken for granted. By way of example, Linear B sign-sequence *pa-te* can be restored as both πάντες /pántes/ 'all' and πατήρ /patēr/ 'father', based on Linear B orthographic conventions.[75] This shows that one and the very same sign-sequence lends itself to being 'restored' (hence read and interpreted) in different ways (based on context). If this equally holds true for Linear A, a number of different 'readings' can be given to Linear A sign-sequences: a circumstance which has often produced the misguided outcome of deeming Linear A as 'a good fit' for several (even unrelated) target languages based on preferential readings (and restorations) of its sign-sequences. Moreover, another problem with the etymological method is that vocabulary alone is not probative enough for language identification: words can easily be borrowed (as loanwords) from one language to another through language contact.

To avoid the pitfalls of misguided, unfounded or misleading interpretations, in a pioneering article Duhoux (1998: 34–5) outlined a theoretical eleven-step methodology for a sound investigation of an undeciphered script as challenging (both contextually and linguistically) as Linear A, with a view to leading to convincing decipherment. This is also known as 'Duhoux's methodology for decipherment' (see e.g. Davis 2014: 10–13) and is centred around the following guidelines (here summarised): using only correctly edited Linear A texts (e.g. *GORILA*) as primary sources, which clearly distinguish between phonetic and ideographic signs; giving sound methodological justifications for Linear A signs' phonetic readings; reconstructing the phonological, morphological and syntactical systems of the Minoan language based on text-internal patterns; reconstructing Linear A orthographic conventions as accurately as possible; ensuring that the identified patterns (grammatical, orthographic) *do* occur systematically and regularly across texts; and ensuring that interpretations of Minoan words are compatible with the archaeological and historical contexts (and not anachronistic). A convincing decipherment shall satisfy all these requirements, and as a result it should explain the majority of the Linear A lexicon in a consistent fashion, allowing for an accurate interpretation of all texts (even the most complex). Duhoux's principles are objective and still observed as theoretical guidelines for decipherment.

Another method to recover meaning is comparative palaeographic analysis between related scripts, which has been done for Linear A and Linear B, given their historical development (see Sections 1 and 4). A good number of Linear

---

[75] See esp. Melena 2014a–b; Salgarella 2023.

A signs' phonetic values could be surmised by comparison with their Linear B counterparts, or 'descendants', as it were. There are contextual, historical reasons legitimising the validity of adopting this approach for the Aegean Linear scripts (see lastly Steele and Meissner 2017). However, the proviso needs adding that this is not to be taken as a blanket approach universally applicable to script decipherment in any context.

Textual and internal analysis (textual structure) of Linear A texts, also known as the context-based 'combinatorial' method, has proved more promising than the etymological method to shed light on the characteristics of the Minoan language. This contextual approach consists in studying the textual structure of Linear A documents (see also Section 6.1.1) to infer the potential meaning of signs (especially ideograms and transaction terms) and sign-sequences (words) by identifying systematic patterns and assessing contextual cues. This method has been systematically and convincingly adopted by John Younger (2024, *Linear A Texts: Introduction*), Ilse Schoep (esp. Schoep 2002) and Brent Davis (Davis 2014). This method allows us to deduce the (at least approximate) meaning of words without necessarily knowing the underlying language. For instance, given that the word *KU-RO* tends to occur at the end of a list and is followed by the total number of the commodities listed in the preceding entries, it is highly likely it means something like 'total/sum' (see also Section 8.2).

Recently, a novel methodology for investigating Linear A (and also, more broadly, all undeciphered Aegean scripts) has been explored by Brent Davis. This is called 'syllabotactic' analysis:[76] a linguistics-based and statistics-based Linear A system-internal and syllable-specific (i.e. 'syllabotactic') analysis of sounds' constraints and words' positions. It consists in using phonotactic and syllabotactic constraints (which govern the ways in which phones and syllables are arranged into words in a given language and are thus language-specific) as investigative tools to examine the linguistic features of the Minoan language, and also whether Bronze Age Aegean scripts encode the same or different languages. Davis' research sits at the forefront of linguistic analyses of Linear A and the Minoan language, and is expected to produce intriguing and exciting results (some of which have already been appreciated in the academic community).

Lastly, digital and statistical analyses may also help in deciphering Linear A and/or shedding light on the nature of the Minoan language (one limitation being the reasonably small size and repetitive nature of the Linear A corpus) by detecting meaningful recurrent structures and clusterings that may escape the human eye (as already pinpointed by Packard 1968, 1971). This is a pathway of

---

[76] Presented in Davis 2018; further applied in Davis forthcoming; Davis in press.

research which is the next *desideratum* in the field, and will necessarily require significant interdisciplinary and multidisciplinary collaborations.

By combining the methodologies and approaches illustrated above, and integrating the ensuing results, we have thus arrived at 'reading' Linear A to a great extent and making sense of a good number of texts (see Section 7). Although Linear A cannot be purported to be fully 'deciphered' yet, we can say (with good reason) that it is at least 'partially deciphered': on present knowledge, it is a matter of 'degree of decipherment'. So, let us now briefly review what is known of the Minoan language.

8.1 Phonology

Phonology studies languages' sound systems: the set of sounds (phones) that are meaningful within a language system (phonemes) and which sound combinations are permitted. Although we do not have an in-depth understanding of the exact phonemic and phonetic repertory of the Minoan language, we can 'read' Linear A by applying Linear B phonetic values to homomorph Linear A–Linear B signs (see Sections 4 and 7). The assumption underpinning this approach is that if the graphic shape of a given sign was continued from Linear A to Linear B, the same or an approximate phonetic value was also maintained – even more so because the Linear A to Linear B script adaptation process took place within the circumscribed context of the administrative practice. The most comprehensive investigation of the Linear A phonological system is carried out by Davis (2014: 192–278; in press).

On present knowledge, Linear A is understood to have five vowels (complete syllabic series for /a/, /i/, /u/, while incomplete for /e/, /o/) and twelve consonantal series (surmised by comparison with Linear B), including stops (/p/, /t/, /k/, voicing and aspiration unclear; plus a separate series for /d/), nasals (/n/, /m/), liquids (/l/, /r/, represented by the same consonantal series, standardly transcribed as *r*-series in both Linear A and Linear B), fricative (/s/), approximants (/w/, /j/), affricates (*z*-series) and labio-velars (*q*-series) of much-debated phonetic interpretation. Several Linear A syllabograms show a subscript number (e.g. *PA$_2$*, *PA$_3$*, etc.), which indicates an allophonic (i.e. phonetic variation) reading of said syllabogram. Reconstructing the sound system of the Minoan language (as attempted by Duhoux 1992: 74–9; Davis 2014: 192–278; Consani 2021: 50–3) may well be purported to be the thirteenth Labour of Herakles, an arduous task to say the least and far from being fully accomplished.

8.2 Morphology

Morphology studies the principles governing word formation (words' internal structure). Only very few Minoan words are known to us, either because they survived into Mycenaean and/or alphabetic Greek or because their meaning can be inferred from their contextual position in Linear A inscriptions (textual-internal analysis). Let us have a look at what this 'Pocket Minoan Dictionary' contains.

On Linear B tablets we find a number of place-names that appear to be non-Greek (non-Indo-European) and may be thought to belong in the Minoan substratum, as they occur with almost the same spelling in Linear A. For example, Linear A *DI-KI-TE* (PK Za 11a, *GORILA* IV: 32) 'Mount Dikte' (cf. Linear B *di-ka-ta-de* and ethnic adjective *di-ka-ta-jo*, *DMic* ss.vv.); Linear A *PA-I-TO* (HT 120.6, *GORILA* I: 204) 'Phaistos' (cf. Linear B *pa-i-to*, *DMic* s.v.); Linear A *TU-RU-SA* (KO Za 1b, *GORILA IV:* 18) 'Tylissos' (cf. Linear B *tu-ri-so*, *DMic* s.v.); Linear A *I-DA* (PK Za 18, *GORILA* IV: 44) 'Mount Ida' (cf. Linear B ethnic adjective *i-da-i-jo*, *DMic* s.v.); Linear A *SE-TO-I-JA* (PR Za1.b, *GORILA* IV: 46) unidentified location, perhaps Arkhanes or Mallia (cf. Linear B *se-to-i-ja*, *DMic* s.v.).

We also know the Minoan words for 'wool' and 'fig'. The word for 'wool' is most likely concealed behind the Linear A monogram *MA+RU* (corresponding to composite sign A 559; see Section 4, Figure 5), used as ideogram for 'wool' and continued in Linear B with the same function (Linear B sign *145/*LANA*): the Minoan word for 'wool' is likely to have been borrowed into Greek as μαλλός /mallós/ 'wool/fleece' (Hesiod uses μαλλός /mallós/ for 'fleece' in *Works and Days* 234; Hesychius preserves the gloss μάλλυκες /mállukes/ explained as the word for τρίχες /trík^{h}es/ on Crete). The word for 'fig' is likely to have survived into Greek as νικύλεον /nikúleon/ (Neumann 1958, 1962). Linear A sign AB 30, read as /ni/ and used as ideogram for 'fig', is likely to be the acrophonic abbreviation of νικύλεον /nikúleon/. In Linear A another word for 'fig' is also attested: *KI-KI-NA* (HT 88.2, *GORILA* I: 138) 'figs of sycamore' (Neumann 1960; cf. Greek κεικύνη /keikúne/, glossed by Hesychios as σοκάμινος /sokáminos/ 'fruit of the sycamore'). As a proviso, although these are likely to be Minoan words, extra care needs to be exercised when working on vocabulary, as words are easily borrowable (esp. in case of cultural and linguistic contact).[77]

Linear A transaction terms (see also Section 4), identified through contextual and text-internal analysis, are another group of words whose meaning can be inferred from their contextual occurrences. Among these, the most securely identified are the following (Schoep 2002: 159–66; Younger 2024, *Linear A Lexicon*):

- *KU-RO* 'total' (HT 9a.6, 9b.6, *GORILA* I: 18), *PO-TO-KU-RO* 'grand total' (HT 122b.6, *GORILA* I: 208), perhaps also *KU-RA* 'total' (ZA 20.4, *GORILA*

---

[77] On non-Indo-European borrowings into Greek, see esp. Renfrew 1998.

III: 192) and *DA-I* 'total' (HT 12.6, *GORILA* I: 24); *KI-RO* 'deficit/owed' (HT 123a.9, *GORILA* I: 210), perhaps also *U-MI-NA-SI* 'owed' (HT 28b.1–2: *GORILA* I: 52)

- *A-DU* 'assessment' (HT 95b.1, *GORILA* I: 154), also occurring as a prefix (e.g. *A-DU-RE-ZA*, *A-DU-KU-MI-NA*, of unknown meaning)
- *KA-I-RO* 'balance' (ZA 8.6, *GORILA* III: 164), perhaps also *KI-RA* 'balance' (HT 103.5, *GORILA* I: 170)

A few word-endings have been identified in Linear A, primarily by comparison with Linear B, as a number of personal names appear in both scripts (showing morphological adaptation to Greek in Linear B; see Steele and Meissner 2017): for example, Linear A *DI-DE-RU* (HT 86a.3, *GORILA* I: 134) and *PA-JA-RE* (HT 88.4, *GORILA* I: 138) correspond to Linear B *di-de-ro* (KN Dv 1504B, *DMic* s.v.) and *pa-ja-ro* (KN As 1519.6, *DMic* s.v.), showing the Greek *-os* masculine ending. Hence, Minoan *-RU* and *-RE* are likely to be the Minoan language counterparts of Greek *-os*.

Moreover, in Linear A we see a consistent use of affixes (i.e. prefixes and suffixes) for word formation (Duhoux 1978): these are usually individual syllables added at word-start or word-end to convey additional information (which could be gender, number, etc.). The following affixes have been identified:

- *TE/-TI* (suffix) 'from' or 'of' (Valério 2007): for example, *A-TU-RI-SI-TI* (KN Zb 5, *GORILA* IV: 76; prefixed with *A-* of unknown function) 'from' *TU-RU-SA* 'Tylissos' (KO Za 1b, *GORILA IV:* 18), and *RI-RU-MA-TI* (PH 31b.4, *GORILA* I: 318) 'from' *RI-RU-MA* (HT 118.4, *GORILA* I: 200)
- *I-/J-* (prefix) 'to' or 'at' (Duhoux 1997): for example, *I-PA-SA-JA* (KH 10.3, *GORILA* III: 36) 'to/at' *PA-SE-JA* (HT Wc 3001–2, *GORILA* II: 72), and *JA-SA-SA-RA-ME* (object case, see Section 7.2)

In Linear A the suffix *-JA* is also likely to be used to form adjectives (Younger 2024, *Linear A Texts: Introduction*, section 13, 'Grammar'). Since in Linear B we find the ethnic adjective *su-ki-ri-ta-jo* 'Sybritan' (derived from place-name *su-ki-ri-ta* 'Sybris'),[78] which also occurs in Linear A with a comparable spelling (*SU-KI-RI-TE-I-JA*, incised before firing on a pithos found at Haghia Triada: HT Zb 158b, *GORILA* IV: 65; cf. place-name *SU-KI-RI-TA* on a nodule from Phaistos: PH Wa 32, *GORILA* II: 90), the assumption can be made that the suffix *-JA* was used for adjectival formation. Comparable instances (Linear A-only) are *PA-SA-RI-JA* (HT 24a.4, *GORILA* I: 42) and *KU-PA$_3$-RI-JA* (HT 24a.1, *GORILA* I: 42), possibly related to place-names *PA-SE-JA* (HT 93a.8, *GORILA* I: 146) and *KU-PA-RI* (PE 1.1–2; see Section 6.1.1, Figure 6), respectively.

---

[78] Compare, e.g., alphabetic Greek forms Σύβριτος, Σίβρυτος, Σούβριτα (see McArthur 1993: 147).

8.3 Syntax

Syntax studies the principles governing sentence formation. Given the nature of the extant evidence (Sections 2 and 3), Linear A texts display very little syntax. The longest inscriptions displaying syntactical structures come from cultic contexts (ritual vessels), among which the libation formula (see Section 7.2) plays a major role in reconstructing the Minoan syntactical system. We thus need to be mindful that context (limited, formulaic sample of inscriptions for cultic/ritual use; e.g. dedications, invocations, prayers) may to some extent bias our overall understanding of Minoan syntax. Based on an analysis of the libation formula (Duhoux 1992; Davis 2013, 2014; see Section 7.2), it has been suggested (Davis 2013) that Minoan may be a Verb-Subject-Object (VSO) language, meaning that the verb is placed at the start of a sentence, followed by the subject and object. In language typology, this is a marked word order. (English is a Subject-Verb-Object (SVO) language: 'Lucy reads a book'). Interestingly, all known verb-initial languages of Eurasia and north Africa are of Verb-Subject-Object type (Dryer 2008; Davis 2013: 49), although this is not enough probative evidence to claim an affiliation of Minoan with any of these languages.

8.4 What Language, Then?

At this point, we shall pose the burning question yet again: what language does Linear A encode? By applying the etymological method (whose pitfalls have already been pointed out), scholars have proposed an affiliation of Minoan with Semitic languages (esp. Gordon 1966, 1969; Best 1972, 2001), Anatolian Indo-European languages (esp. Palmer 1958, 1968; Finkelberg 1990–1; Brown 1990, 1993; Renfrew 1998; Owens 2000), or even Greek (Georgiev 1963, 1968a–b; Nagy 1963, 1965; Tsikritsis 2000). Minoan has also been argued to be related to Hurrian (esp. Monti 2002, 2005, 2006; van Soesbergen 2017), Etruscan (esp. Facchetti 2001; Facchetti and Negri 2003) or Hattic/Hatto-Sumerian (Schrijver 2018). Other proposals have also been advanced (see Davis 2014: 190 for further references).

However, despite the current advances in the understanding of Minoan grammar (esp. syntax) by combining and integrating complementary approaches (e.g. combinatorial, statistical, syllabotactic), there is not yet enough data (nor corroborating enough) incontrovertibly to identify the linguistic affiliation (if any) of the Minoan language (as summarised in Davis 2014: 279–80). The data retrieved from an integrated analysis of the extant evidence suggests that the Minoan language does not belong in any known language family (the families so far used for comparative purposes being Indo-European, Semitic, Afro-Asiatic; see esp. Davis 2014: 156–278; Davis in press; Davis forthcoming; Duhoux 2020), and is therefore to be taken as an 'isolated' language, indigenous to Crete. The high use of affixes (esp. multisyllabic prefixes) suggests that Minoan is an agglutinative language (or a language showing agglutinative tendencies) rather than inflective (Duhoux 1978), and that affixes may play an important role in expressing syntactic relations (also gender, case or derivation; Schoep 2002: 45–6).

How much (more?) Minoan shall we expect to know in the foreseeable future? New pathways of research (see Section 10) are key to extracting more (and meaningful) data from the limited, concise evidence at our disposal. The application of digital approaches to the Linear A corpus is a huge *desideratum*,[79] which requires extensive multi-disciplinary collaborations between humanities and sciences, and may have the strong potential to shed more light on the distinctive characteristics of the Minoan language.

Yet, is decipherment the only goal? Perhaps not (necessarily). By integrating the aforementioned methods and placing the Linear A inscribed documents within their archaeological setting and against their socio-historical backdrop, we can retrieve a considerable amount of information to reconstruct the workings of Minoan administration and economy, as well as getting insights into society, contemporary cultural dynamics, interactions and contacts. If our goal is to draw as accurate a socio-historical reconstruction as possible of the Minoan civilisation (of which language is a constitutive component, but not the only one), then we are on the right path without necessarily having yet reached a 'full-decipherment'. In other words, there is plenty of information we can extract from both the archaeological and written records, beyond linguistic decipherment *stricto sensu*.

9 More Unresolved Mysteries: What Do We Not Have in Linear A?

Another challenge we face is 'managing absence'. There are no surviving literary texts of any genre written in Linear A (historiography, poetry, treatises, etc.), nor diplomatic correspondence, monumental inscriptions, private letters or the like: anything that does not fall (more or less neatly) within the remits of either administration or cultic activity is missing. A legitimate question springing to mind is: would we expect this evidence? Also in this case, there is no short answer (nor uncontroversial).

9.1 Likely *Yes*

There is indirect evidence for the use of perishable materials as writing supports, leading us to assume (speculatively and cautiously) that perhaps more extensive writings falling outside the administrative sphere *stricto sensu* did exist (e.g.

---

[79] For example, Nakassis and Pluta (2003) demonstrate the viability of applying multidimensional scaling to Linear A tablets and texts.

historiography, literature, diplomatic correspondence, private documents, etc.). But these writings did not survive: the very same conflagrations responsible for baking the Linear A clay documents (and thus preserving them until today) incinerated writings on perishable material (e.g. parchment, papyrus).

Our best (indirect) evidence for perishable materials used as writing supports are two typologies of clay sealings: flat-based nodules and single-hole hanging nodules, both used to authenticate records, secure their integrity and prevent unauthorised viewing (see Sections 5.2, 5.3 and 6.1.2). Flat-based nodules show string imprints on their undersides (while seal impressions on the front),[80] suggesting they were pressed against tightly folded sheets of parchment (or, more loosely, leather) tied with a string (Figure 14; see also *CMS* II, 6 pp. 350–7; Hallager 1996: 140; Montecchi 2019: 247–70). Flat-based nodules are attested as early as the Proto-Palatial period and are common to both Cretan Hieroglyphic and Linear A administrative systems (Hallager 1996: 39–74, 135–6, 230–1), but are not continued into Linear B administration. Single-hole hanging nodules likely (or *possibly*) hung

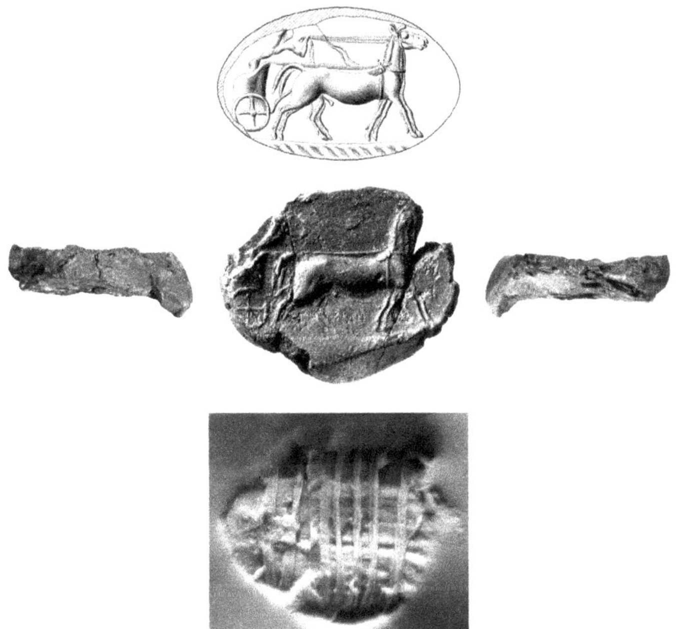

Figure 14 Flat-based nodule showing string imprints on the underside.[81]

---

[80] On Aegean seals, see esp. Krzyszkowska 2005; Karnava 2018.

[81] Karnava 2018: 258, N1/MPTh A8888. Image courtesy of Akrotiri Excavations Archives/CMS Heidelberg.

from strings tied to (papyrus?) rolls: imprints of the string passing through their top-hole are in fact still visible at times (Hallager 1996: 135–45, 197–9; Tomas 2010: 124; Montecchi 2019: 270–97). This category of sealings is a new introduction in the Linear A administrative practice, but did not continue into Linear B (as there is no indirect evidence for the use of perishable materials in Linear B; see esp. Palaima 2011: 124).

Likely to be placed in archives to be consulted at need, this evidence may have contained information we do not find on Linear A tablets (which we *may* expect, especially by comparison with Near-Eastern administrative practices) – for example, laws, decrees, balances from previous years, landholdings, diplomatic correspondence and so on. It is worth noting that, in the more extensive Linear B clay documents, these categories of texts are not evident either (except for landholdings and a reference to a possible legal 'dispute'). Writing supports like parchment/leather sheets (and papyrus rolls), which were obliterated by fire destructions (see Section 2), may have contained longer texts (esp. if written on both sides) compared to short and concise clay tablets. The existence of perishable materials brings up the question of the extent of literacy in Minoan Crete, which is still (partially) *terra incognita*.

9.2 Likely *No*

Another group of document types is unlikely to have existed, as there is neither direct nor indirect evidence thereof (and, if there were, it should be somewhat visible in the archaeological record). These are monumental inscriptions in durable materials (comparable to those we see in Egypt and the Near-East), temple/wall inscriptions, celebratory inscriptions, funerary inscriptions and so forth, just to name a few. We may wonder why this is so: is it yet another unanswerable question on present knowledge (and evidence)? A suggestion has been made (Bennet 2018) to explain the apparent lack of 'monumental' inscriptions in the Bronze Age Aegean context: the function of such classes of textual evidence may have been fulfilled by a different, complementary yet not overlapping communicative strategy (which does not necessarily presuppose, or necessitate, writing), namely participatory practices of enacted performances within the context of a much broader cultural literacy (comprising visual, textual and performative elements), encompassing archaeologically intangible performative aspects and practices. Hence, shall we expect more evidence to be unearthed in the foreseeable future? Or else, shall we 'expect' this evidence ever to be found or, more precisely, ever to have existed? Perhaps only posterity will judge.

All in all, the extant written evidence represents only a small window on what we can reconstruct of 'Minoan' writing practices. What has survived the chances of time may not necessarily give us a complete and all-encompassing picture of 'Minoan' writing practices, some of which are inferable only indirectly (e.g. the extent and nature of writing on perishable material). Speculations and inferences aside, it is also true that, even if we had all that had not survived, the full array of writing activities in Minoan Crete may not have been as wide/comprehensive as in the neighbouring Egyptian and Near-East contexts for the unquestionable lack, at least on present evidence, of certain types of writing media and contexts (above all, monumental inscriptions).

9.3 Who Wrote the Linear A Inscriptions?

Differently put, where are the Linear A 'scribes'? Almost nothing is known of the individuals responsible for writing the Linear A inscriptions that have survived to us. This is due to a variety of reasons. First, as far as we know, Linear A 'writers' never signed the texts they produced (neither the records of economic transactions for the bookkeeping of contemporary palatial administrations, nor the dedicatory prayers/formulas used for cultic activity), nor did any 'writer' ever identify themselves as 'author' in any of the extant (textual or archaeological) sources (in stark contrast to, e.g., ancient Mesopotamia, where even female scribes signed their texts). Second, we do not have any additional literary evidence (e.g. poetry, private correspondence, funerary inscriptions, etc.), contemporary historical documents (treatises, decrees, diplomatic correspondence, etc.) or iconographic sources, either from within the Aegean or from neighbour societies, providing details about (or displaying visual evidence of) Linear A 'writers'. Third, in the archaeological record, there is no straightforward nor incontrovertible evidence of materials and/or contexts that can be associated with Linear A 'writers' (e.g. places where 'scribal activity' may have taken place, 'scribal schools' or 'workshops', etc.).[82] Hence we cannot make (often automatic and implicit) assumptions about Linear A writers' gender and biological sex, age, social status, occupation (or 'profession' in more modern terminology), just to name a few.

In recent Aegean scholarship (esp. in Linear B studies) and current academic discourse, the more neutral terms 'scribal hand' and 'writer' are preferred over the traditional, more marked term 'scribe', which is too often

---

[82] On activities of Linear A 'scribes', Schoep (2002: 187) mentions the instance of correspondence between 45 *noduli* and tablet HT 24 (dealing with wool) near the southwestern entrance to the Villa at Haghia Triada (Room 26), which might give an indication of practice (see also Palaima 1994: 118; Hallager 1996: 132; del Freo 2020). This is the only arguable instance of a tablet found in its primary context (i.e. where it was presumably written), since most Linear A 'deposits' are the locations where tablets were kept after they had been written (see also fn. 41).

implicitly associated with Egyptian and Near-Eastern writing contexts and practices, where the role of 'scribes' is more clearly defined (and identifiable as such). In traditional Aegean scholarship, the assumption is often made that Aegean 'writers' also fulfilled the role of palatial administrators (esp. in the Mycenaean context) and are therefore implicitly expected to be men, to the point that in most academic papers Aegean 'writers' are (still) referred to as 'scribes' and addressed by 'he/his' pronouns. Only a few scholars (e.g. Kyriakidis 2011; Judson 2020) have now started to use more neutral phrasing ('(s)he' or 'they') to address Aegean (Linear B) 'writers'. As for the Minoan (Linear A) context, the traditional assumption about 'male scribes' is not substantiated by any kind of probative evidence and must therefore be considered unfounded for the time being (especially on considering that we have examples of fully trained women 'scribes' in Sippur and Mesopotamia; see e.g. Lion 2009). Hence, on present evidence and state of the art, it is clearly not possible to identify most of the characteristics that we often (implicitly) associate with ancient inscription writers.

Moreover, very little research has been conducted so far on Linear A 'writers', mostly because of the nature of the Linear A evidence (paucity and quality; see Section 8), but also because of the lack of appropriate, reliable and necessary research tools for sound palaeographic analysis and statistical cross comparison of inscriptions' handwriting. A few scholars (Raison and Pope 1971; *GORILA* V: 83–113; Militello 1989; Schoep 1996; Tomas 2011b; Montecchi 2019) attempted to identify and single out Linear A 'scribal hands' (to use traditional terminology), but most works focus on Haghia Triada, which contains the highest number of Linear A administrative documents (see Section 3). Unveiling details of the individuals hidden behind the Linear A inscriptions is an exciting research avenue that necessitates interdisciplinary collaborations and the development of new research tools. This research may give us valuable insights into literacy (and the extent thereof) in the Bronze Age 'Minoan' context.

10 Current and Future Pathways of Research: What's Next?

Although most (and most reliable) material on Linear A is only available in institutional and university libraries and academic databases, in recent years there have been a number of projects disseminating (textual and photographic) material to a wider, educated (yet not necessarily specialist) audience. This section gives an outline of the resources currently available online (often under ongoing development), hoping that their number will steadily increase over time, thanks to international interdisciplinary collaborations between scholars, museums and institutions, and the use of novel digital technologies.

10.1 Online Resources

• Standard corpus of Linear A inscriptions: ***GORILA***

Black-and-white sans of the traditional corpus of Linear A inscriptions (*GORILA*, five volumes) are available online on the website of the publishers (at http://cefael.efa.gr/result.php?site_id=1&serie_id=EtCret), under 'Études Crétoises 21' (items 17–21).
A supplementary volume is published by Del Freo and Zurbach (2025).
The complete standardised list of Linear A signs is given in *GORILA*, Volume V, pp. xxii–xxviii.

• Collected papers on Linear A: **John Younger's writings**

John Younger's writings (from his former website *Linear A Texts & Inscriptions in Phonetic Transcription & Commentary*, www.academia.edu/117949876/ Linear_A_Texts_and_Inscriptions_in_phonetic_transcription, University of Kansas) are available to download (in PDF format) on Younger's Academia. edu webpage (http://kansas.academia.edu/JYounger).

• Bibliographical database: ***Nestor***

Nestor is an online international bibliographical database of Aegean studies, Homeric society, Indo-European linguistics and related fields, published by the Department of Classics, University of Cincinnati (http://classics.uc.edu/ nestor/).

10.2 Towards Digital Corpora of Inscriptions

• Palaeographical database of Linear A inscriptions: *SigLA*

SigLA – The Signs of Linear A: A Palaeographical Database (Salgarella and Castellan 2020; Salgarella and Castellan 2021) is a user-friendly, interactive database containing line drawings of most Linear A administrative documents and a Linear A sign list. *SigLA* is open access at http://site.unibo.it/ inscribe/en/linear-a-sigla and http://sigla.phis.me.

• Three-dimensional models of Linear A inscriptions

The *INSCRIBE Project* (S. Ferrara, University of Bologna) produced 3D models of a number of Linear A inscriptions, which can be viewed at http://inscribercproject.com/Linear_A.php.

• RTI and three-dimensional models of Linear A sealings and tablets

The pa-i-to Epigraphic Project (A. Greco, La Sapienza University of Rome; G. Flouda, Heraklion Archaeological Museum; E. Notti, IULM University) produced RTI (Reflectance Transformation Imaging) images and three-dimensional models of a number of Linear A clay sealings and tablets, which can be viewed at http://paitoproject.it/en/pa-i-to-project-2/.

References

Bendall, L. M. (2017). Where was da-wo? In M.-L. Nosch and H. Landenius Enegren, eds., *Aegean Scripts: Proceedings of the 14th International Colloquium on Mycenaean Studies, Copenhagen, 2–5 September 2015*, vol. 1. Rome: Consiglio Nazionale delle Ricerche, pp. 301–45.

Bennett, E. L., Jr. (1963). Names for Linear B writing and for its signs. *Kadmos* 2(2), 98–123.

Bennet, J. (1992). 'Collectors' or 'owners'? An examination of their possible functions within the palatial economy of LMIII Crete. In J.-P. Olivier, ed., *Mykenaïka. Actes du IXe Colloque international sur les textes mycéniens et égéens, Centre de l'Antiquité Grecque et Romaine de la Fondation Hellénique des Recherches Scientifiques et École française d'Athènes.* Paris: Diffusion de Boccard, pp. 65–101.

(1999). The meaning of 'Mycenaean': Speculations on ethnicity in the Aegean Late Bronze Age. *BICS*, 43, 224.

(2002). Millennial ambiguities. In Y. Hamilakis, ed., *Labyrinth Revisited. Rethinking 'Minoan' Archaeology.* Oxford: Oxbow Books, pp. 214–25.

(2008). Now you see it; now you don't! The disappearance of the Linear A script on Crete. In J. Baines, J. Bennet and S. Houston, eds., *The Disappearance of Writing Systems. Perspectives on Literacy and Communication.* London: Equinox, pp. 1–29.

(2018). Gelb and Gell in the Aegean: Thoughts on the relations between 'writing' and 'art'. In A. R. Knodell and Th. P. Leppard, eds., *Regional Approaches to Society and Complexity: Studies in Honor of John F. Cherry.* Sheffield: Equinox, pp. 59–74.

Best, J. G. P. (1972). *Some Preliminary Remarks on the Decipherment of Linear A.* Amsterdam: Adolf M. Hakkert.

(1990). Traces of Luwian dialect in Cretan texts and toponym. *Studi Micenei ed Egeo-Anatolici*, 28, 225–37.

(1993). The Linear A signary: Tokens of Luwian dialect in Bronze Age Crete. *Minos*, 27–8, 25–54.

(1997). Linear A on Trojan spindlewhorls, Luvian-Based WANAX at Cnossus. In G. Schmeling and J. D. Mikalson, eds., *Qui miscuit utile dulci: Festschrift Essays for Paul Lachlan MacKendrick.* Wauconda, IL: Bolchazy-Carducci, pp. 51–68.

(2001). The first inscription in Punic: Vowel differences in Linear A and B. *Ugarit-Forschungen*, 32, 27–35.

Chadwick, J. (1967). *The Decipherment of Linear B. . .* Cambridge: Cambridge University Press.

CHIC = Olivier, J.-P. and Godart, L., eds. (1996). *Corpus Hieroglyphicarum Inscriptionum Cretae*. Paris: de Boccard.

Civitillo, M. (2016). *La scrittura geroglifica minoica sui sigilli: Il messaggio della glittica protopalaziale*. Pisa: Fabrizio Serra Editore.

Cline, E. H., ed. (2010). *The Oxford Handbook of the Bronze Age Aegean (ca. 3000–1000 BC)*. Oxford: Oxford University Press.

CMS I-XIII = Matz, F., Biesantz, H., Pini, I. and Muller, W., eds. (1964–2009). *Corpus der minoischen und mykenischen Siegel*, vols. I–XIII. Berlin and Mainz: Gebruder Mann and Philipp von Zabern.

Consani, C. (2021). *Studi e Saggi Linguistici*, 59(1), 25–74.

Coulmas, F. (2003). *Writing Systems: An Introduction to Their Linguistic Analysis*. Cambridge: Cambridge University Press.

Davis, B. (2013). Syntax in Linear A: The word-order of the 'libation formula'. *Kadmos*, 52(1), 35–52.

(2014). *Minoan Stone Vessels with Linear A Inscriptions*. Leuven: Peeters.

(2018). The Phaistos Disk: A new way of viewing the language behind the script. *Oxford Journal of Archaeology*, 37(4), 373–410.

(in press). *Form without Meaning: Linguistic Investigations into the Undeciphered Aegean Scripts*. Cambridge: Cambridge University Press.

(forthcoming). Recent linguistics-based advances in the study of Linear A. In E. Salgarella and V. Petrakis, eds., *The Wor(l)ds of Linear A: Interdisciplinary Approaches to Documents and Inscriptions of a Cretan Bronze Age Script*. Athens: University of Athens Press.

Decorte, R. P.-J. E. (2018a). The first 'European' writing: Redefining the Archanes script. *Oxford Journal of Archaeology*, 37(4), 341–72.

(2018b). The origins of Bronze Age Aegean writing: Linear A, Cretan Hieroglyphic and a new proposed pathway of script formation. In S. Ferrara and M. Valério, eds., *Paths into Script Formation in the Ancient Mediterranean*. Rome: Edizioni Quasar di Severino Tognon, pp. 13–49.

de Fidio, P. (2024). The absolute values of the symbols for volume. In J. T. Killen, ed., *The New Documents in Mycenaean Greek*, vol. 1. Cambridge: Cambridge University Press, pp. 169–204.

Del Freo, M. (2005). Le scritture egee del II millennio: rassegna dei materiali epigrafici e considerazioni storiche. *Rendiconti Lincei*, 16(4), 633–8.

(2020). Wool working at Hagia Triada: The HT 24 tablet and the 45 noduli from the Quartiere Sudovest. In B. Davis and R. Laffineur, eds., *Νεώτερος:*

Studies in Bronze Age Aegean Art and Archaeology in Honor of Professor John G. Younger on the Occasion of His Retirement. Leuven: Peeters, pp. 55–63.

Del Freo, M. and Zurbach, J. (2011). La préparation d'un supplément au Recueil des inscriptions en linéaire A. Observations à partir d'un travail en cours. *Bulletin de Correspondance Hellénique*, 135(1), 73–97.

Del Freo, M. and Zurbach, J. 2025. Recueil des inscriptions en linéaire A. Supplément 1. École française d'Athénes.

Dimopoulou, N., Olivier, J.-P. and Réthémiotakis, G. (1993). Une statuette en argile MR IIIA de Poros Irakliou avec inscription en linéaire A. *Bulletin de Correspondance Hellénique*, 117, 501–21.

Dimopoulou-Rethemiotaki, N. (2005). *The Archaeological Museum of Herakleion*. Athens: EFG Eurobank Ergasias S. A. and John S. Latsis Public Benefit Foundation.

DMic = Aura Jorro, F. and Adrados, F. R., eds. (1985–93). *Diccionario Micénico*. Vol. 1 (1985), Vol. 2 (1993). Madrid: Consejo Superior de Investigaciones Científicas.

Donnelly, C. M. (2022). Cypro-Minoan and its potmarks and vessels inscriptions as challenges to Aegean Scripts corpora. In P. M. Steele and P. J. Boyes, eds., *Writing around the Ancient Mediterranean: Practices and Adaptations*. Oxford: Oxbow, pp. 49–73.

Driessen, J. (2000). *The Scribes of the Room of the Chariot Tablets at Knossos: Interdisciplinary Approach to the Study of a Linear B Deposit*. Salamanca: Ediciones Universidad de Salamanca.

Driessen, J. and Langohr, C. (2007). Rallying round a 'Minoan' past: The legitimation of power at Knossos during the Late Bronze Age. In M. L. Galaty and W. A. Parkinson, eds., *Rethinking Mycenaean Palaces II*, 2nd ed. Los Angeles: University of California, pp. 178–89.

Dryer, D. (2008). Order of subject, object and verb. In M. Haspelmath, M. S. Dryer, D. Gil and B. Comrie, *World Atlas of Language Structures Online* (https://wals.info/index), section 18.

Duhoux, Y., ed. (1978). *Études minoennes I: Le linéaire A*. Louvain: Peeters.

(1992). Variations morphosyntaxiques dans les textes votifs linéaires A. *Cretan Studies*, 3, 65–88.

(1998). Pre-Hellenic language(s) of Crete. *Journal of Indo-European Studies*, 26, 1–39.

(2020). Minoan Language or Languages? In B. Davis and R. Laffineur, eds., Νεώτερος: *Studies in Bronze Age Aegean Art and Archaeology in Honor of Professor John G. Younger on the Occasion of His Retirement*. Leuven: Peeters, pp. 15–21.

Elvira Astoreca, N. (2021). *Early Greek Alphabetic Writing: A Linguistic Approach*. Oxford: Oxbow Books.

Evans, A. J. (1921–35). *The Palace of Minos: A Comparative Account of the Successive Stages of the Early Cretan Civilization as Illustrated by the Discoveries at Knossos*, 6 vols. London: Macmillan.

Evely, D. (2000). *Minoan Crafts: Tools and Techniques. An Introduction. Part Two*. Upsala: Åströms Förlag.

Facchetti, G. M. (2001). Qualche osservazione sulla lingua minoica. *Kadmos*, 40, 1–38.

Facchetti, G. M. and Negri, M. (2003). *Creta Minoica: Sulle tracce delle più antiche scritture d'Europa*. Firenze: Olschki.

Ferrara, S. (2015). The beginnings of writing on Crete: Theory and context. *British School at Athens*, 110, 27–49.

Ferrara, S., Montecchi, B. and Valério, M. (2021a). The making of a script: Cretan Hieroglyphic and the quest for its origins. *Bulletin of the American Schools of Oriental Research*, 386, 1–22.

(2021b). What is the 'Archanes Formula'? Deconstructing and reconstructing the earliest attestation of writing in the Aegean. *British School at Athens*, 116, 43–62.

Finkelberg, M. (1990–1). Minoan inscriptions on libation vessels. *Minos*, 25–6, 43–85.

Finkelberg, M., Uchitel, A. and Ussishkin, D. (1996). A Linear A inscription from Tel Lachish (Lach ZA 1). *Tel Aviv*, 23, 195–207.

Finlayson, S. (2013). Form follows function: Writing and its supports in the Aegean Bronze Age. In K. E. Piquette and R. D. Whitehouse, eds., *Writing as Material Practice: Substance, Surface and Medium*. London: Ubiquity Press, pp. 123–42.

(2018). Little things in a big landscape: Thoughts on the mobility of sealings and sealing practices in First and Second Palace Period Crete. In Μιτσοτάκη, Κλαίρη and Λένα Τζεδάκη-Αποστολάκη, eds., *Πεπραγμένα ΙΒ΄ Διεθνούς Κρητολογικού Συνεδρίου, Ηράκλειο, 21–25 Σεπτεμβρίου 2016 / Proceedings of the 12th International Congress of Cretan Studies*. Ηράκλειο: Εταιρία Κρητικών Ιστορικών Μελετών – Ιστορικό Μουσείο Κρήτης, pp. 1–10.

(2020). The House Seal: Examining seal use and sealing practices in Proto- and Neopalatial Crete in the light of Lévi-Strauss' Model of House Societies. In M. Relaki and J. Driessen, eds., *Oikos. Archaeological approaches to House Societies in the Bronze Age Aegean*. Louvain-la-Neuve: Presses universitaires de Louvain, pp. 185–200.

Flouda, G. (2013). Materiality of Minoan writing: Modes of display and perception. In K. E. Piquette and R. D. Whitehouse, eds., *Writing as Material Practice: Substance, Surface and Medium*. London: Ubiquity Press, pp. 143–74.

(2015). Materiality and script: Constructing a narrative on the Minoan inscribed axe from the Arkalochori Cave. *Studi Micenei ed Egeo-Anatolici*, New Series 1, 43–56.

Galanakis, Y. (2015). 'Islanders vs. Mainlanders', 'The Mycenae Wars', and other short stories: An archival visit to an old debate. In J. L. Davis and V. Florou, eds., *Carl W. Blegen: Personal and Archaeological Narratives*. Atlanta: Lockwood Press, pp. 99–120.

(2022). Neither Minoan nor Mycenaean: The burial record of Knossos and the materialisation of a new social order, 1600–1400. In A. L. D'Agata, L. Girella, E. Papadopoulou and D. G. Aquini, eds., *One State, Many Worlds: Crete in the Late Minoan II–IIIA2 Early Period. Proceedings of the International Conference held at Chania, Μεγάλο Αρσενάλι, 21st–23rd November 2019*. Rome: Edizioni Quasar, pp. 139–78.

Georgiev, V. (1963). Les deux langues des inscriptions crétoises en linéaire A. *Linguistique Balkanique*, 7(1), 1–104.

(1968a). L'état actuel du déchiffrement des textes en linéaire A. In *Atti e Memorie del 1°Congresso Internazionale di Micenologia*. Rome: Edizioni dell'Ateneo, pp. 355–82.

(1968b). Quand les Grecs sont-ils venus en Crète? In *Pepragmena tu B' Diethnus Kritoloyiku Sinedriu 2*. Athens: Filoloyikos Sillogos 'O Hrisostomos', pp. 40–3.

Godart, L. (1984). Du Lineaire A au Lineaire B. In *Aux origines de l'Hellénisme. La Crète et la Grèce. Hommage à Henri van Effenterre présenté par le Centre G. Glotz*. Paris: Université de Paris I Panthéon-Sorbonne, pp. 121–8.

Gordon, C. H. (1966). *Evidence for the Minoan Language*. Ventnor: Ventnor Publishers.

(1969). Minoan. *Athenaeum*, 47(1–4), 125–35.

GORILA = Godart, L. and Olivier, J.-P. (1976–85). *Recueil des inscriptions en Linéaire A*, 5 vols. Paris: Librairie Orientaliste Paul Geuthner.

Hallager, E. (1990). Roundels among sealings in Minoan administration: A comprehensive analysis of function. In Th. G. Palaima, ed., *Aegean Seals, Sealings and Administration. Proceedings of the NEH-Dickson Conference of the Program in Aegean Scripts and Prehistory of the Department of Classics, University of Texas at Austin, January 11–13, 1989*. Liège: Université de Liège, pp. 121–48.

(1996). *The Minoan Roundel and Other Sealed Documents in the Neopalatial Linear A Administration*, 2 vols. Liège: Université de Liège.

(2010). Development of sealing practices in the Neopalatial Period. In W. Müller, ed., *Die Bedeutung der minoischen und mykenischen Glyptik: VI. Internationales Siegel-Symposium aus Anlass des 50 jährigen Bestehens des CMS, Marburg, 9.–12. Oktober 2008*. Mainz am Rhein: Verlag Philipp von Zabern, pp. 205–12.

(2021). The Minoan roundel: Its function, seals and inscriptions. *Pasiphae*, 15, 189–97.

Hallager, E. and Hallager, B. P., eds. (2016). *The Greek-Swedish Excavations at the Agia Aikaterini Square, Kastelli, Khania, 1970–1987, 2001, 2005 and 2008: Results of the Excavations under the Direction of Yannis Tzedakis and Carl-Gustaf Styrenius*. Stockholm: Svenska Institutet i Athen.

Halstead, P. (1995). Late Bronze Age grain crops and Linear B ideograms *65, *120, and *121. *British School at Athens* 90, 229–34.

Hamilakis, Y. (2002). What future for the Minoan past? Re-thinking Minoan archaeology. In Y. Hamilakis, ed., *Labyrinth Revisited: Rethinking 'Minoan' Archaeology*. Oxford: Oxbow Books, pp. 2–28.

Houston, S. D., ed., (2004). *The First Writing: Script Invention as History and Process*. Cambridge: Cambridge University Press.

Judson, A. P. (2017). The decipherment: People, process, challenges. In A. Christophilopoulou, Y. Galanakis and J. Grime, eds., *Codebreakers & Groundbreakers*. Cambridge: Charlesworth Press, pp. 15–29.

(2020). Scribes as editors: Tracking changes in the Linear B documents. *American Journal of Archaeology*, 124(4), 523–49.

Kanta, A., Nakassis, D., Palaima, Th. G. and Perna, M. (2024). An archaeological and epigraphical overview of some inscriptions found in the Cult Center of the city of Knossos (Anetaki plot). In J. Bennet, T. Meissner and A. Karnava, eds., *KO-RO-NO-WE-SA. Proceedings of the 15th International Colloquium on Mycenaean Studies September 2021*. Rethymnon: Faculty of Philosophy, University of Crete, pp. 27–43.

Karadimas, N. and Momigliano, N. (2004). On the term 'Minoan' before Evans's work in Crete (1894). *Studi Micenei ed Egeo-Anatolici*, 46, 243–58.

Karetsou, A., Godart, L. and Olivier, J.-P. (1985). Inscriptions en linéaire A du sanctuaire de sommet minoen du mont Iouktas. *Kadmos*, 24(2), 89–147.

Karnava, A. (2016). On sacred vocabulary and religious dedications: The Minoan 'libation' formula. In E. Alram-Stern, F. Blakolmer, S. Deger-Jalkotzy, R. Laffineur and J. Weilhartner, eds., *Metaphysis: Ritual, Myth and Symbolism in the Aegean Bronze Age. Proceedings of the 15th International Aegean Conference, Vienna, Institute for Oriental and*

European Archaeology, Aegean and Anatolia Department, Austrian Academy of Sciences and Institute of Classical Archaeology, University of Vienna, 22–25 April 2014. Leuven and Liège: Peeters, pp. 345–55.

(2018). *Seals, Sealings and Seal Impressions from Akrotiri in Thera*, CMS Beiheft 10. Heidelberg: CMS Heidelberg/Propylaeum Heidelberg University Library.

Killen, J. T. (2004). Wheat, barley, flour, olives and figs on Linear B tablets. In P. Halstead and J. C. Barrett, eds., *Food, Cuisine and Society in Prehistoric Greece*. Oxford: Oxbow Books, pp. 155–73.

Killen, J. T., ed. (2024a). *The New Documents in Mycenaean Greek*. Cambridge: Cambridge University Press.

Killen, J. T. (2024b). Agricultural produce. In J. T. Killen, ed., *The New Documents in Mycenaean Greek, Volume 2*. Cambridge: Cambridge University Press, pp. 533–64.

Kopaka, C. 1989. Une nouvelle inscription en linéaire A de Zakros. *Kadmos*, 28(1), 7–13.

Kyriakidis, E. (2011). The smell of big cheese: Perfume production and the differing spheres of influence of high scribes H1 and H2 at Pylos. *Pasiphae*, 5, 127–39.

Krzyszkowska, O. (2005). *Aegean Seals: An Introduction*. London: Institute of Classical Studies.

Lion, B. (2009). Les femmes scribes de Sippar. *Topoi. Orient-Occident, Supplément* 10, 289–303.

Macdonald, C. F. and Knappett, C. (2007). *Knossos: Protopalatial Deposits in Early Magazine A and the South-West Houses*. London: The British School at Athens.

McArthur, J. K. (1993). *Place-Names in the Knossos Tablets. Identification and Location*. Salamanca: Ediciones Universidad de Salamanca.

Meissner, T. and Salgarella, E. (2024). The relationship between Cretan Hieroglyphic and the other Cretan Scripts. In M. Civitillo, S. Ferrara and T. Meissner, eds., *Cretan Hieroglyphic*. Cambridge: Cambridge University Press, pp. 134–64.

Melena, J. L. (2014a). Mycenaean writing. In Y. Duhoux and A. Morpurgo Davies, eds., *A Companion to Linear B: Mycenaean Greek Texts and Their World, Volume 3*. Louvain-la-Neuve and Walpole, MA: Peeters, pp. 1–186.

(2014b). Filling gaps in the basic Mycenaean syllabary. In A. Bernabé and E. R. Luján, eds., *Donum Mycenologicum: Mycenaean Studies in Honour of Francisco Aura Jorro*. Louvain-la-Neuve and Walpole, MA: Peeters, pp. 75–85.

Militello, P. (1989). Gli scribi di Haghia Triada. Alcune osservazioni. *La Parola del Passato*, 44, 126–47.

Montecchi, B. (2010). A classification proposal of Linear A tablets from Haghia Triada in classes and series. *Kadmos*, 29, 11–38.

(2017). Classification, use, and function of hanging nodules in the Neopalatial administrative practices (Minoan Crete). *Archäologischer Anzeiger*, 2017(1), 1–18.

(2018). Mobility to, from and within Neopalatial Crete: The evidence from the sealings. In Μιτσοτάκη, Κλαίρη and Λένα Τζεδάκη-Αποστολάκη, eds., *Πεπραγμένα ΙΒ΄ Διεθνούς Κρητολογικού Συνεδρίου, Ηράκλειο, 21–25 Σεπτεμβρίου 2016 / Proceedings of the 12th International Congress of Cretan Studies*. Ηράκλειο: Εταιρία Κρητικών Ιστορικών Μελετών – Ιστορικό Μουσείο Κρήτης, pp. 1–12.

(2019). *Contare a Haghia Triada: Le tavolette in lineare A, i documenti sigillati e il sistema economico-amministrativo nel TM IB*. Rome: CNR Edizioni.

Monti, O. (2002). Observations sur la langue du Linéaire A. *Kadmos*, 41, 117–20.

(2005). Considérations sur quelques termes des textes votifs linéaires A. *Kadmos*, 44, 19–22.

(2006). Observations sur quelques termes linéaires A. *Kadmos*, 45, 69–72.

(2015). Linéaire B da-wo et la datation de la tablette KN F(2) 852+. *Kadmos*, 54(1–2), 23–30.

(2019). Linéaire B da-wo: indiquait-il Kommos ou Haghia Triada? *Kadmos*, 58(1–2), 93–110.

Morris, Ch. (2017). Minoan and Mycenaean figurines. In T. Insoll, ed., *The Oxford Handbook of Prehistoric Figurines*. Oxford: Oxford University Press, pp. 659–79.

Nagy, G. (1963). Greek-like elements in Linear A. *Greek, Roman and Byzantine Studies*, 4, 181–211.

(1965). Observations on the sign-grouping and vocabulary of Linear A. *American Journal of Archaeology*, 69, 295–330.

Nakassis, D. and Pluta, K. (2003). Linear A and multidimensional scaling. In K. P. Foster and R. Laffineur, eds., *Metron: Measuring the Aegean Bronze Age. Proceedings of the 9th International Aegean Conference / 9e Rencontre égéenne internationale, New Haven, Yale University, 18–21 April 2002*. Belgium: Université de Liège, Histoire de l'art et archéologie de la Grèce antique; University of Texas at Austin, Program in Aegean Scripts and Prehistory, pp. 335–42 (with Plates LXVI–LXVII).

Neumann, G. (1958). Zwei minoische Gefassbezeichnungen. *Glotta*, 37, 106–12.

(1960). Minoisch kikina 'die Sykomorenfeige. *Glotta*, 38, 181–6.

(1962). Nikuleon. *Glotta*, 40, 51–4.

(1996). A Linear A inscription from Miletus (MIL Zb 1). *Kadmos*, 35, 87–99.

Oren, E. D. (1996). Minoan Graffito from Tel Haror (Negev, Israel). *Cretan Studies*, 5, 91–118.

Owens, G. (2000). Pre-Hellenic language(s) of Crete: Debate and discussion. *Journal of Indo-European Studies*, 28(1–2), 237–53.

Packard, D. W. (1968). Contextual and statistical analysis of Linear A. In *Atti e Memorie del 1°Congresso Internazionale di Micenologia*. Rome: Edizioni dell'Ateneo, pp. 389–94.

(1971). Computer techniques in the study of the Minoan Linear Script A. *Kadmos*, 10(1), 52–9.

Palaima, Th. G. (1987). Comments on Mycenaean literacy. In J. T. Killen, J. L. Melena and J-P. Olivier, eds., *Studies in Mycenaean and Classical Greek Presented to John Chadwick*. Minos 20–22. Salamanca: Universidad de Salamanca, pp. 499–510.

(1994). Seal-Users and Script-Users/Nodules and Tablets at LM IB Hagia Triada. In P. Ferioli, E. Fiandra, G. G. Fissore and M. Frangipane, eds., *Archives before Writing: Proceedings of the International Colloquium Oriolo Romano, October 23–25, 1991*. Rome: Centro Internazionale di Ricerche Archeologiche Antropologiche e Storiche, pp. 307–30.

(2003). The inscribed bronze 'kessel' from Shaft Grave IV and Cretan heirlooms of the bronze artist named 'Aigeus' vel sim. in the Mycenaean Palatial Period. In Y. Duhoux, ed., *Briciaka: A Tribute to W. C. Brice*. Amsterdam: Adolf M. Hakkert, pp. 187–201.

(2011). Scribes, scribal hands and palaeography. In Y. Duhoux and A. Morpurgo Davies, eds., *A Companion to Linear B: Mycenaean Greek Texts and Their World, Volume 2*. Leuven: Peeters, pp. 33–136.

(2020). Problems in Minoan and Mycenaean writing style and practice: The strange case of *33 ra₃ on Pylos tablet Aa 61. In B. Davis and R. Laffineur, eds., Νεώτερος. *Studies in Bronze Age Aegean Art and Archaeology in Honor of Professor John G. Younger on the Occasion of His Retirement*. Leuven and Liège: Peeters, pp. 3–14.

Palmer, L. R. (1958). Luvian and Linear A. *Athenaeum*, 46, 431–4.

(1968). Linear A and the Anatolian languages. In *Atti e Memorie del 1°Congresso Internazionale di Micenologia*. Rome: Pubblicazioni dell'Ateneo, 339–54.

Palmer, R. (1992). Wheat and barley in Mycenaean society. In J.-P. Olivier, ed., *Mykenaïka: Actes du IXe Colloque international sur les textes mycéniens et égéens, Centre de l'Antiquité Grecque et Romaine de la Fondation*

Hellénique des Recherches Scientifiques et École française d'Athènes.
Paris: Diffusion de Boccard, pp. 475–97.

(2008). How to begin? An introduction to Linear B conventions and resources. In Y. Duhoux and A. Morpurgo Davies, eds., *A Companion to Linear B: Mycenaean Greek Texts and Their World, Volume 1*. Leuven: Peeters, pp. 25–68.

Peatfield, A. and Morris, Ch. (2020). Peak sanctuary figurines: Materialising issues of ritual personhood within community/house identity. In M. Relaki and J. Driessen, eds., *Oikos. Archaeological Approaches to House Societies in the Bronze Age Aegean*. Louvain-la-Neuve: Presses universitaires de Louvain, pp. 173–83.

Pelon, O. (1980). *Le palais de Malia*. Paris: Librairie Orientaliste Paul Geuthner.

Perseus Digital Library (Tufts University): Open-access at https://www.per seus.tufts.edu/hopper/.

Petrakis, V. (2012). Reverse phonetisation? From syllabogram to sematogram in Aegean scripts. In P. Carlier, C. de Lamberterie, M. Egetmeyer, N. Guilleux, F. Rougemont and J. Zurbach, eds., *Études mycéniennes 2010: Actes du XIIIe colloque international sur les textes égéens, Sèvres, Paris, Nanterre, 20–23 septembre 2010*. Pisa: Fabrizio Serra Editore, pp. 523–36.

(2014). Some notes on the place of ku-do-ni-ja in Late Minoan III political geography. *DO-SO-MO*, 10, 55–80.

(2017). Figures of speech? Observations on the non-phonographic component in the Linear B writing system. In M.-L. Nosch and H. Landenius Enegren, eds., *Aegean Scripts: Proceedings of the 14th International Colloquium on Mycenaean Studies, Copenhagen, 2–5 September 2015*. Rome: Consiglio Nazionale delle Ricerche Edizioni, pp. 127–67.

Piquette, K. E. and Whitehouse, R. D. (2013). Introduction: Developing an approach to writing as material practice. In K. E. Piquette and R. D. Whitehouse, eds., *Writing as Material Practice: Substance, Surface and Medium*. London: Ubiquity Press, pp. 1–13.

Pope, M. (2008). The decipherment of Linear B. In Y. Duhoux and A. Morpurgo Davies, eds., *A Companion to Linear B: Mycenaean Texts and Their World, Volume 1*. Leuven: Peeters, pp. 1–23.

Protonotariou-Deilaki, E. (1990). Burial customs and funerary rites in the Prehistoric Argolid. In R. Hägg and G. C. Nordquist, eds., *Celebrations of Death and Divinity in the Bronze Age Argolid: Proceedings of the Sixth*

International Symposium at the Swedish Institute at Athens, 11–13 June, 1988. Stockholm: Paul Åströms Förlag, pp. 69–83.

Raison, J. and Pope, M. (1971). *Index du Linéaire A*. Rome: Edizioni dell'Ateneo.

(1994). *Corpus transnuméré du linéaire A*, 2nd ed. Louvain-la-Neuve: Peeters.

Renfrew, C. (1998). Word of Minos: The Minoan contribution to Mycenaean Greek and the linguistic geography of the Bronze Age Aegean. *Cambridge Archaeological Journal*, 8(2), 239–64.

Rice, M. (in press). Non-administrative Linear A writing practices: The case of stone vessels (c. 1800–1450 BC). In C. M. Donnelly, ed., *Too Much Writing, Too Few Scribes: Extra-scribal Writing in the Late Bronze Age Mediterranean (1650–1100 BCE)*. Oxford: Archaeopress.

Robinson, A. (2000). *The Story of Writing*. London: Thames and Hudson.

Rogers, H. (2005). *Writing Systems: A Linguistic Approach*. Oxford: Wiley-Blackwell.

Sakellaraki, E., Del Freo, M., Olivier, J.-P. and Zurbach, J. (2018). Une épingle minoenne en argent avec inscription en linéaire A de la tombe à tholos B d'Arkhanès. *Kadmos*, 57(1), 21–32.

Sakellarakis, Y. and Sapouna-Sakellaraki, E., eds. (1997). *Archanes. Minoan Crete in a New Light*. 2 vols. Athens: Ammos.

Salgarella, E. (2019). Drawing lines: The palaeography of Linear A and Linear B. *Kadmos*, 58(2), 61–92.

(2020). *Aegean Linear Script(s): Rethinking the Relationship between Linear A and Linear B*. Cambridge: Cambridge University Press.

(2021). Imagining Cretan scripts: The influence of visual motifs on the creation of script-signs in Bronze Age Crete. *British School at Athens*, 116, 63–94.

(2022a). Linear A. In *The Oxford Classical Dictionary* (digital edition, Oxford University Press).

(2022b). Mix and match: A combinatory re-classification of Linear A signs. *TALANTA*, 54, 31–52.

(2023). Reconstructing a prehistoric writing system. In M. Condorelli and H. Rutkowska, eds., *The Cambridge Handbook of Historical Orthography*. Cambridge: Cambridge University Press, pp. 395–416.

(in press). Material matters: The impact of materiality on the structure of the Linear A script of Bronze Age Crete. In C. Donnelly, ed., *Too Much Writing, Too Few Scribes: Extra-scribal Writing in the Late Bronze Age Mediterranean (1650–1100 BCE)*. Oxford: Archaeopress.

Salgarella, E. and Castellan, S. (2021). SigLA: The Signs of Linear A. A palaeographical database. In Haralambous, Y., ed., *Grapholinguistics in the 21st Century – 2020*. Part II, pp. 945–62. Brest: Fluxus Editions.

Schoep, I. (1995). Context and chronology of Linear A administrative documents. *Aegean Archaeology*, 2, 29–65.

(1996). Minoan administration on Crete: An interdisciplinary approach to documents in Linear A and Cretan Hieroglyphic. Unpublished PhD thesis, Catholic University of Leuven.

(2001). The role of the Linear A tablets in Minoan administration. *Ktèma*, 26, 55–62.

(2002). *The Administration of Neopalatial Crete. A Critical Assessment of the Linear A Tablets and Their Role in the Administrative Process*. Salamanca: Ediciones Universidad de Salamanca.

(2004). The socio-economic context of seal use and administration at Knossos. In G. Cadogan, E. Hatzaki and A. Vasilakis, eds., *Knossos: Palace, City, State: Proceedings of the Conference in Herakleion Organised by the British School at Athens and the 23rd Ephoreia of Prehistoric and Classical Antiquities of Herakleion, in November 2000, for the Centenary of Sir Arthur Evans's Excavations at Knossos*. London: The British School at Athens, pp. 25–6.

(2018). Building the labyrinth: Arthur Evans and the construction of Minoan Civilization. *American Journal of Archaeology*, 122(1), 5–32.

(2020). The development of writing on Crete in EM III–MM IIB (ca. 2200–1750/00 B.C.). In B. Davis and R. Laffineur, eds., *Νεώτερος: Studies in Bronze Age Aegean Art and Archaeology in Honor of Professor John G. Younger on the Occasion of His Retirement*. Leuven and Liège: Peeters, pp. 43–53.

(forthcoming). The impact of the Minoan chronological framework on the study of Minoan and Mycenaean writing and sealing practices. In Salgarella, E. and Petrakis, V., eds., *The Wor(l)ds of Linear A: Interdisciplinary Approaches to Documents and Inscriptions of a Cretan Bronze Age Script*. Athens: University of Athens Press.

Schrijver, P. (2018). Talking Neolithic: The case for Hatto-Sumerian and its relationship to Sumerian. In G. Kroonen, J. P. Mallory and B. Comrie, eds., *Talking Neolithic: Proceedings of a workshop on Indo-European held at the Max Planck Institute for Evolutionary Anthropology, Leipzig, December 2–3, 2013*. Washington, DC: Institute for the Study of Man, pp. 336–74.

Shelmerdine, C. W., ed. (2008). *The Cambridge Companion to the Aegean Bronze Age*. Cambridge: Cambridge University Press.

SigLA = Salgarella, E. and Castellan, C. (2020). *SigLA. The Signs of Linear A: A Palaeographical Database* (open access at www.inscribercproject.com/SigLA/index.html and http://sigla.phis.me).

Steele, P. M. (2023). *Exploring Writing Systems and Practices in the Bronze Age Aegean*. Oxford: Oxbow Books.

Steele, P. M. and Meissner, T. (2017). From Linear B to Linear A: The problem of the backward projection of sound values. In P. M. Steele., ed., *Understanding Relations between Scripts: The Aegean Writing Systems*. Oxford: Oxbow Books, pp. 93–110.

Taylour, W. D. and Janko, R. (2008). *Ayios Stephanos: Excavations at a Bronze Age and Medieval Settlement in Southern Laconia*. London: British School at Athens.

Thompson, R. (2012). In defence of ideograms. In P. Carlier, C. de Lamberterie, M. Egetmeyer, N. Guilleux, F. Rougemont and J. Zurbach, eds., *Études mycéniennes 2010: Actes du XIIIe colloque international sur les textes égéens, Sèvres, Paris, Nanterre, 20–23 septembre 2010*. Pisa: Fabrizio Serra Editore, pp. 545–61.

Tomas, H. (2008). Comparing Linear A and Linear B administrative systems: The case of the roundel and the elongated tablet. In A. Sacconi, M. Del Freo, L. Godart and M. Negri, eds., *Colloquium Romanum: Atti del XII colloquio internazionale di micenologia, Roma, 20–25 febbraio 2006, Volume 2*. Pisa: Fabrizio Serra Editore, pp. 767–74.

(2010). Linear A versus Linear B administrative systems in the sphere of religious matters. In I. Boehm and S. Müller-Celka, eds., *Espace civil, espace religieux en Égée durant la période mycénienne: Approches épigraphique, linguistique et archéologique. Actes des journées d'archéologie et de philologie mycéniennes tenues à la Maison de l'Orient et de la Méditerranée*. Lyon: Maison de l'Orient et de la Méditerranée, pp. 121–33.

(2011a). Linear A tablet ≠ Linear B tablet. In M. Ανδρεαδάκη-Βλαζάκη and Ε. Παπαδοπούλου, eds., *Πεπραγμένα Ι΄ Διεθνούς Κρητολογικού Συνεδρίου, Χανιά, 1–8 Οκτωβρίου 2006, Volume A1*. Χανιά: Φιλολογικός Σύλλογος «Ο Χρυσόστομος», pp. 331–43.

(2011b). Linear A scribes and their writing styles. *Biblioteca di Pasiphae*, 5, 35–58.

(2012). The transition from the Linear A to the Linear B sealing system. In I. Regulski, K. Duistermaat and P. Verkinderen, eds., *Seals and Sealing Practices in the Near East: Developments in Administration and Magic from Prehistory to the Islamic Period. Proceedings of an International Workshop at the Netherlands-Flemish Institute in Cairo on December 2–3, 2009*. Leuven: Peeters, pp. 33–49.

Tsikritsis, M. (2000). Statistiki sygkritikis epexergasias metaxy Grammikis A kai Grammikis B grafis. In A. Karetsou, D. Theocharis and A. Kalokairinos, eds., *Pepragmena H' Diethnous Kritologikou Synedriou, Irakleio, 9–14 Septemvriou 1996, Vol. A3: Proïstoriki kai Archaia Elliniki Periodos.* Irakleio: Etairia Kritikon Istorikon Meleton, pp. 325–58.

Tsipopoulou, M. and Hallager, E. (1996). Inscriptions with hieroglyphs and Linear A from Petras, Siteia. *Studi Micenei ed Egeo-Anatolici*, 37, 7–46.

Valério, M. (2007). 'Diktaian Master': A Minoan predecessor of Diktaian Zeus in Linear A? *Kadmos*, 46, 3–14.

van Soesbergen, P. G. (2017). *Minoan Linear A: Hurrians and Hurrian in Minoan Crete.* 2 vols. Amsterdam: Peter G. Van Soesbergen.

Warren, P. and Hankey, V. (1989). *Bronze Age Chronology.* Bristol: Bristol Classical Press.

Weilhartner, J., ed. (in press). *The Cambridge Companion to Aegean Scripts.* Cambridge: Cambridge University Press.

Weingarten, J. (1986). Some unusual Minoan clay nodules. *Kadmos*, 25, 1–21.

(1990). More unusual Minoan clay nodules: Addendum II. *Kadmos*, 29(1), 16–23.

(2017). When one equals one: The Minoan roundel. In A. M. Jasink, J. Weingarten and S. Ferrara, eds., *Non-Scribal Communication Media in the Bronze Age Aegean and Surrounding Areas: The Semantics of a-Literate and Proto-Literate Media.* Firenze: Firenze University Press, 99–108.

Younger, J. G. (2003). Calculating vessel volumes. In K. P. Foster and R. Laffineur, eds., *Metron: Measuring the Aegean Bronze Age. Proceedings of the 9th International Aegean Conference, Yale University, 18–21 April 2002.* Belgium: Université de Liège, and University of Texas at Austin, Program in Aegean Scripts and Prehistory, pp. 491–2.

(2024). *Linear A Texts and Inscriptions in Phonetic Transcription.* University of Kansas (former website, individual papers currently available as downloadable PDF files on Younger's Academia.edu webpage: http://kansas.academia.edu/JYounger).

Acknowledgements

This Element owes its existence to several scholars, who kindly offered guidance and helped me navigate the challenges posed by the extant Linear A evidence, as well as scholarship. Heartfelt thanks go to Silvia Ferrara for so enthusiastically proposing my name as author for this work, and to Andreas Stauder for his unwavering editorial support and encouragement at all stages of the publication process. Special thanks go to Georgia Flouda for confirming the list of Greek museums currently displaying Linear A evidence, to Maurizio del Freo and Julien Zurbach for confirming the list of Linear A findplaces, to John Younger for sharing with me so generously and promptly the materials once part of his impressive website, to Ilse Schoep for sharing her views and mastery of Linear A so willingly and unreservedly, and, last but not the least, to John Bennet for his ingenious and ever-stimulating comments on various topics covered in this work. I am genuinely thankful for the expertise of Artemis Karnava, Maria Anastasiadou and Sarah Finlayson in seals, sealings and sealing practices, and of Mnemosyne Rice in carving tools. I would also like to extend my heartfelt thanks and gratitude to the two anonymous reviewers of my manuscript for their enthusiastic, detailed and constructive feedback. I wish to extend my most sincere gratitude to the Aarhus Institute of Advanced Studies (AIAS) and the Aarhus Universitet Forskningsfond (AUFF), University of Aarhus (Denmark), where I was based while finalising this work as an AIAS-AUFF Research Fellow. AIAS' intellectually stimulating and engaging interdisciplinary environment gave an edge to the final shape of this work.

For EU product safety concerns, contact us at Calle de José Abascal, 56–1°,
28003 Madrid, Spain or eugpsr@cambridge.org.

www.ingramcontent.com/pod-product-compliance
Ingram Content Group UK Ltd.
Pitfield, Milton Keynes, MK11 3LW, UK
UKHW020319010726
472720UK00010B/386